ISBN: 978-0-9855399-3-1

Published by Zayandeh Publications, New York City
Printed in the United States of America

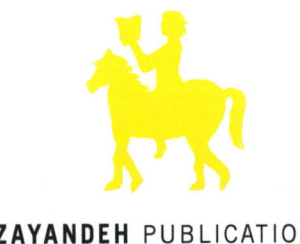

ZAYANDEH PUBLICATIONS

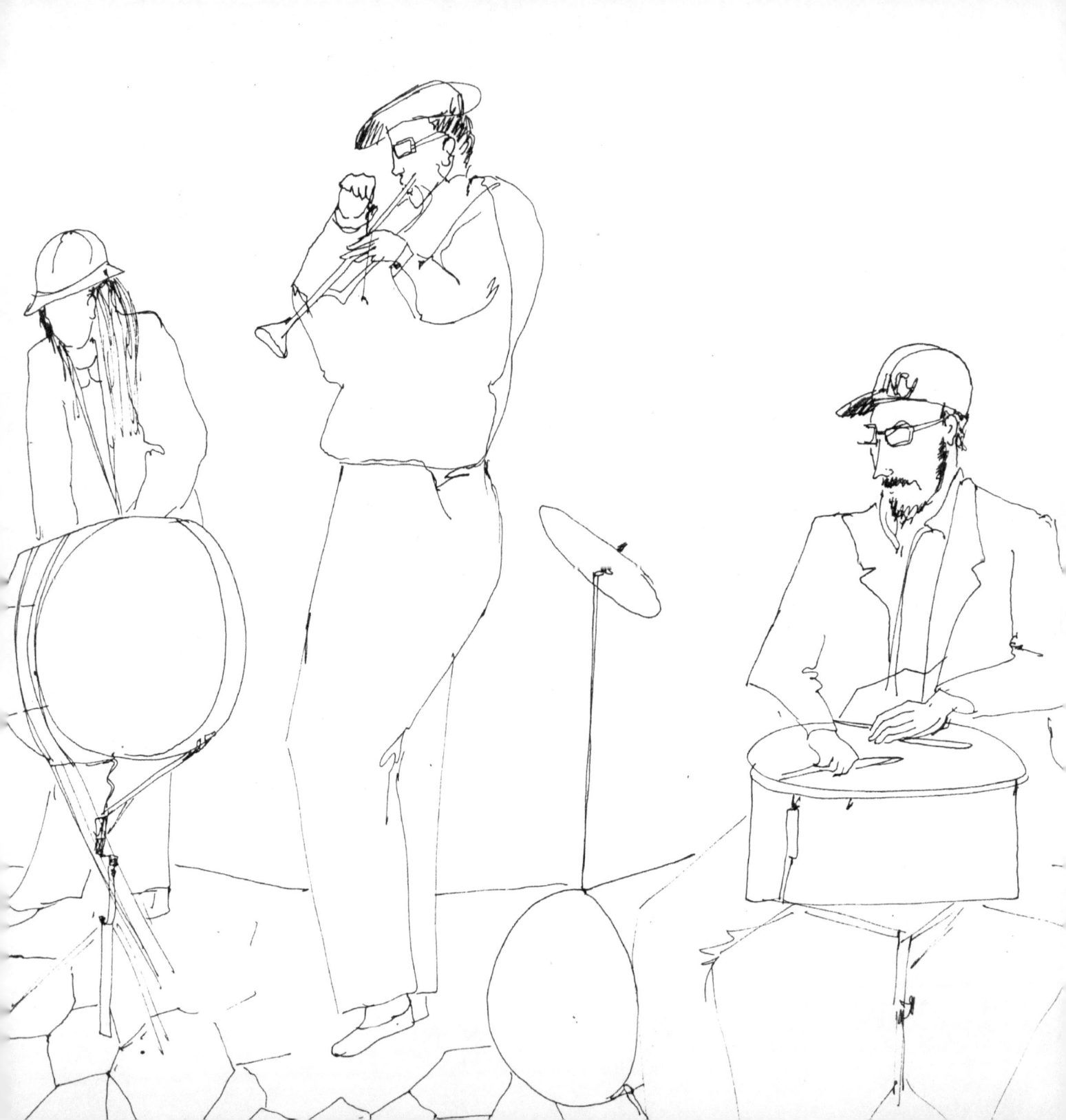

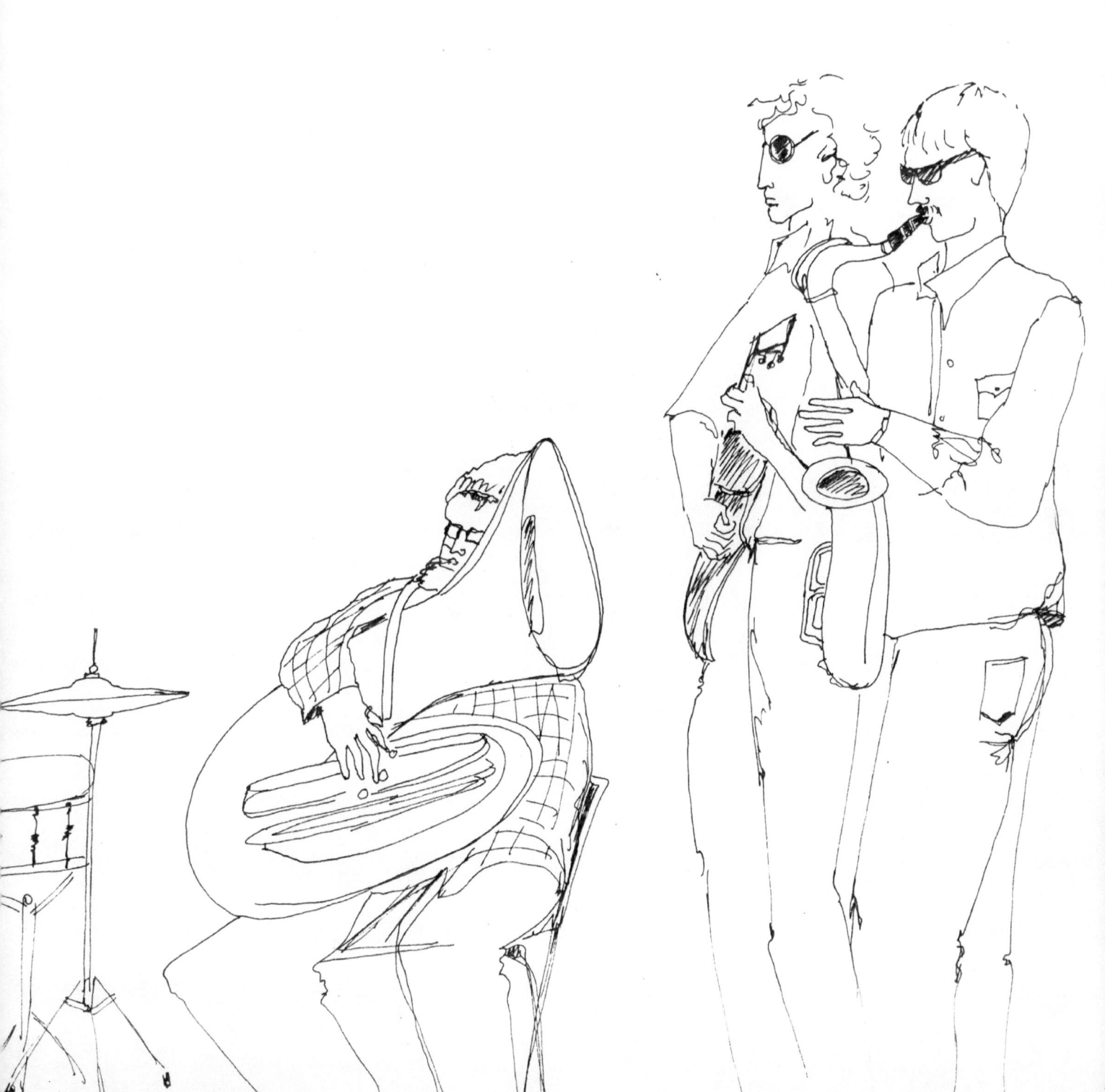

# FACES OF NEW YORK

## Book One

## Manhattan

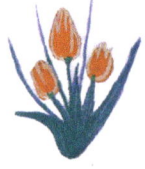

**Mariam Touzie**

Edited by Jancy Ball and Douglas Piccione

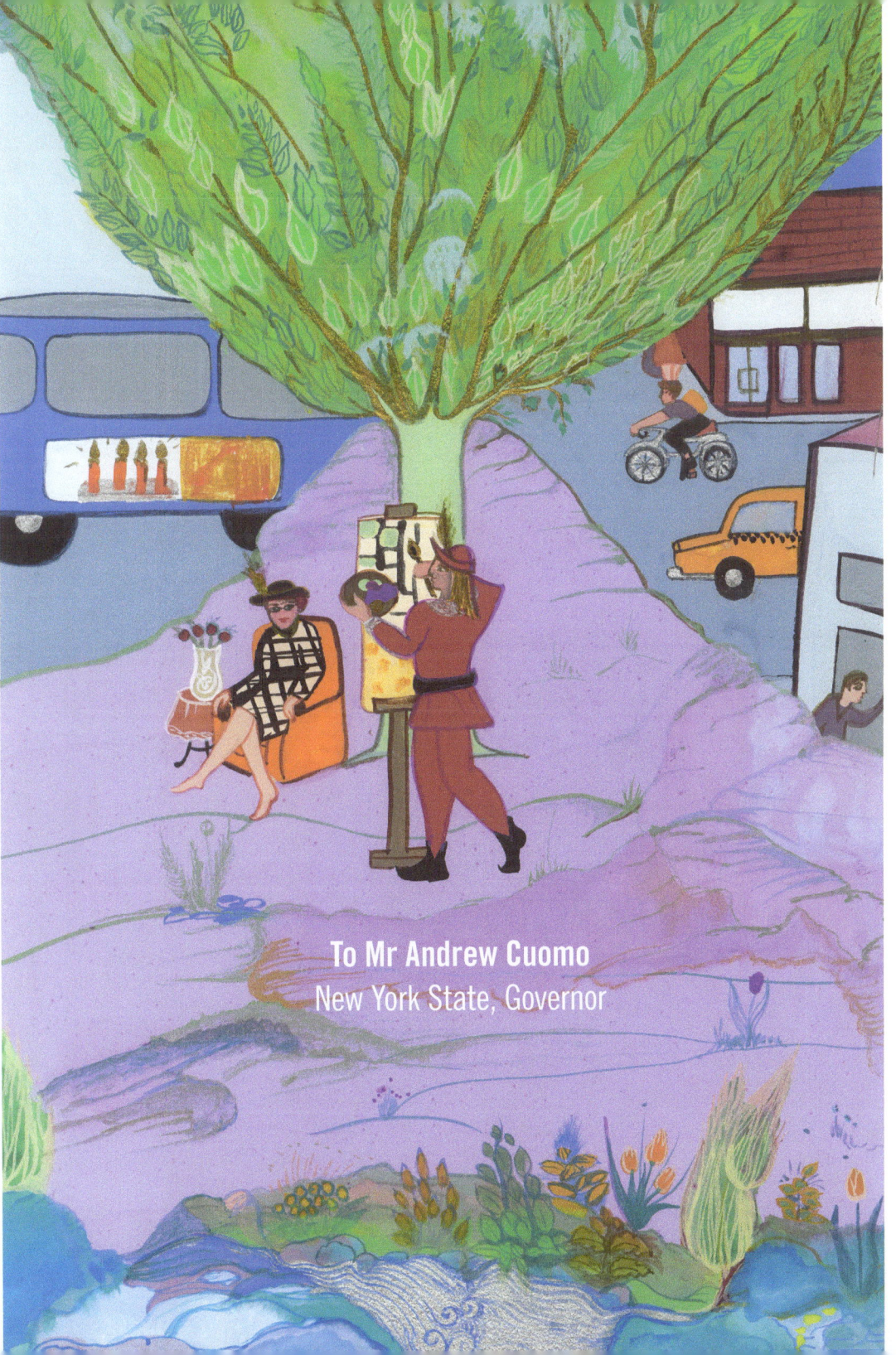

To Mr Andrew Cuomo

New York State, Governor

I was born on the shoulders of the Alborz Mountain in Tehran, Iran.
And never imagined to live decades of my life on an island!

Manhattan is this tiny rock much like a diamond that shines day and night
tucked in the corner of the great Atlantic Ocean.

I've lived on one side or the other of the Empire State Building.
So, I illustrated some of the moments and sights around me since 1986.

Come walk with me through my New York.

—Mariam Touzie
New York City, 2020

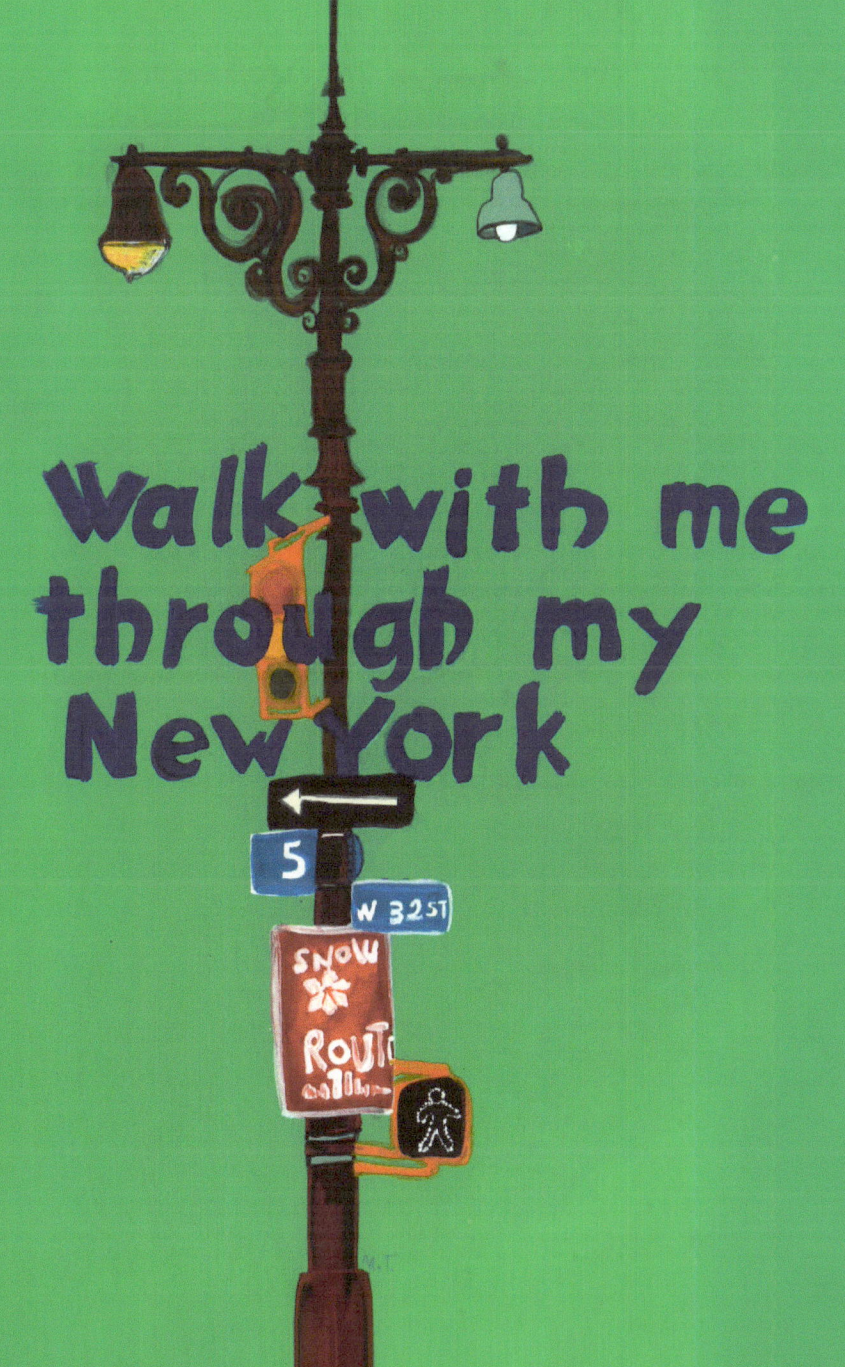

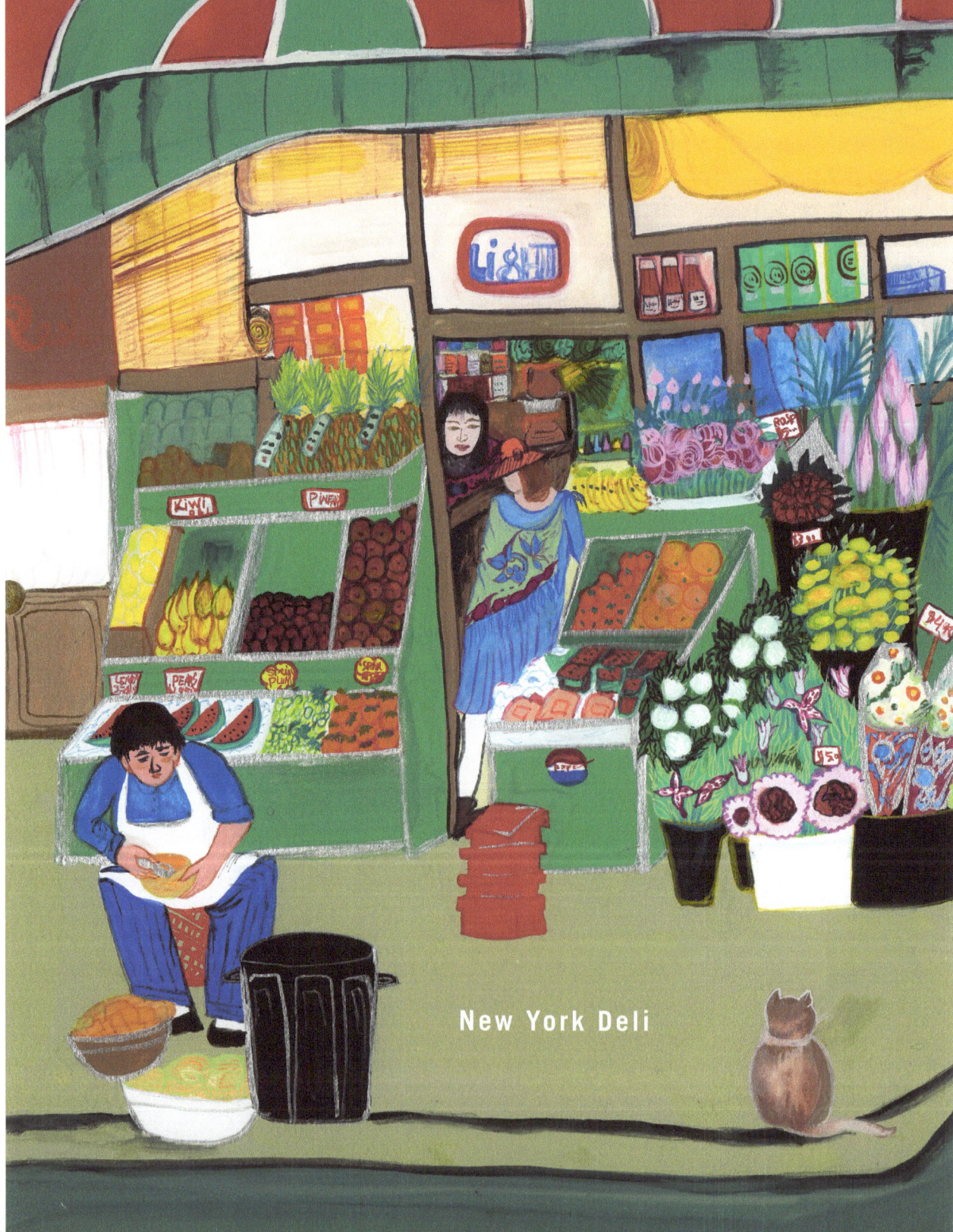

New York Deli

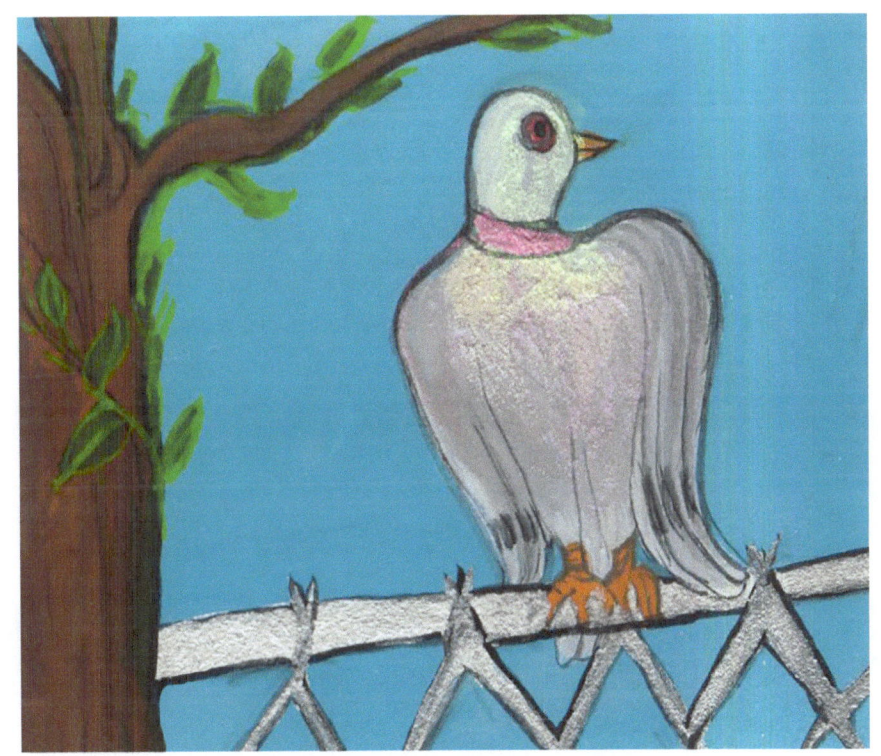

**New York City Pet**

Street Vendors

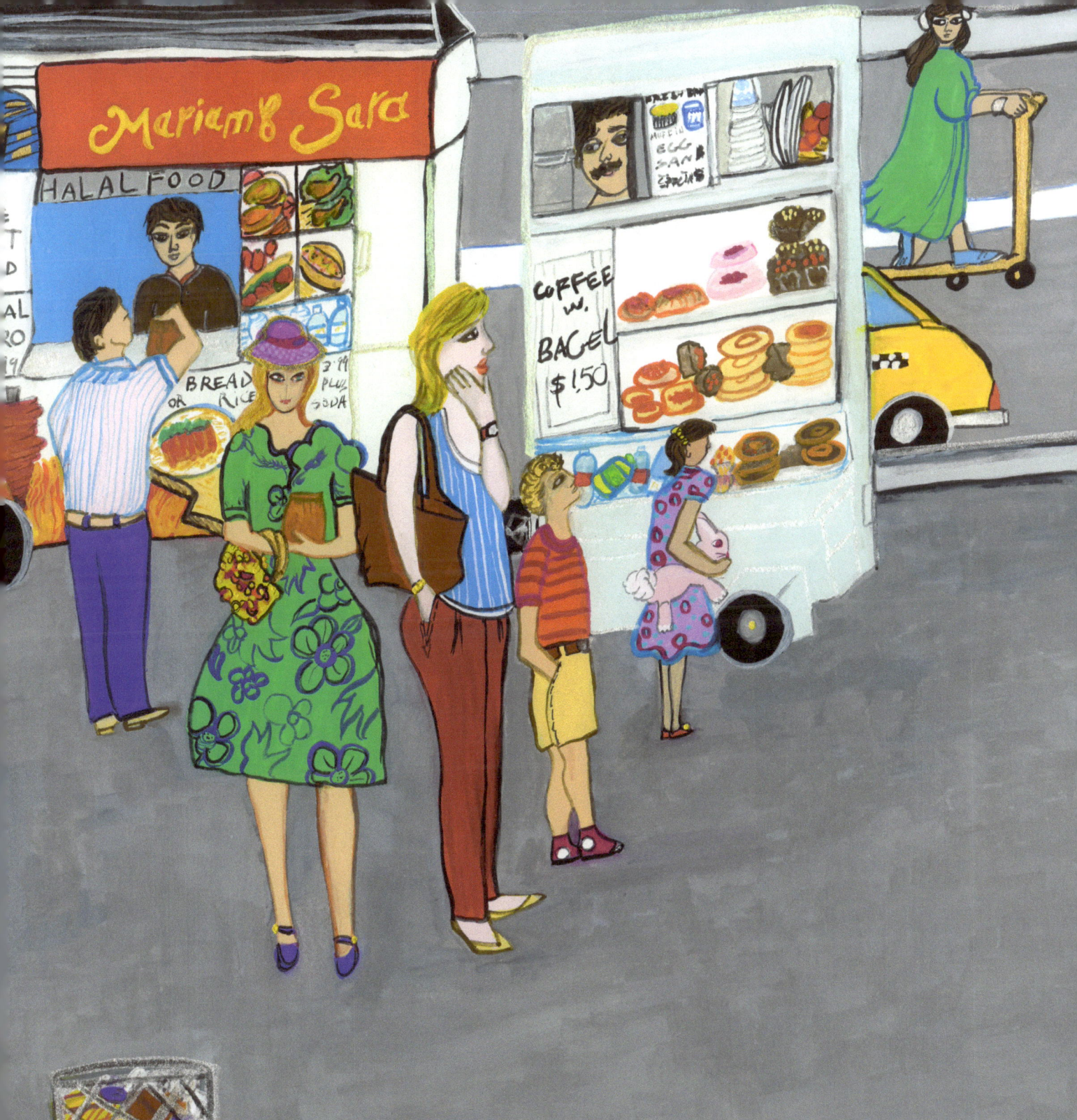

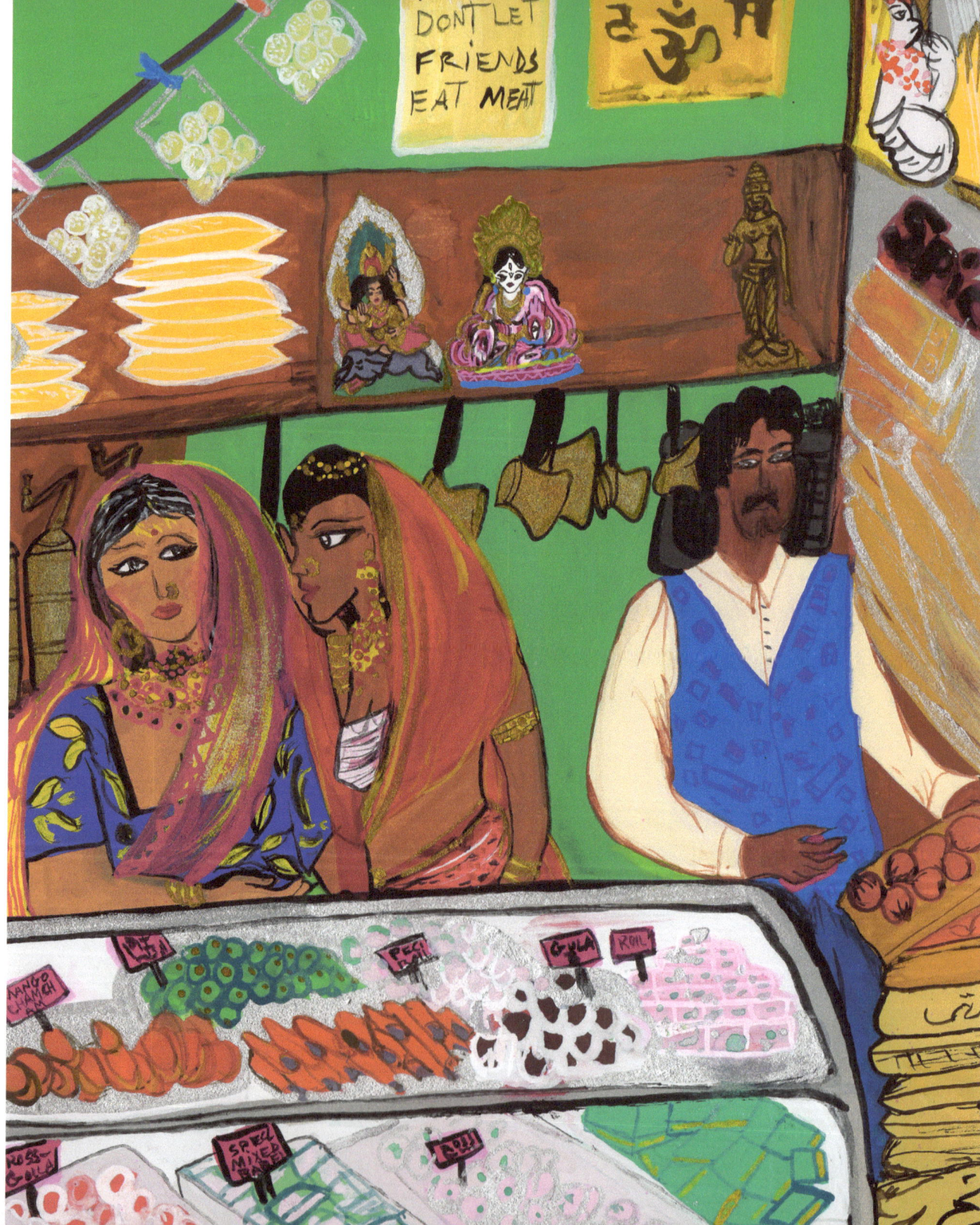

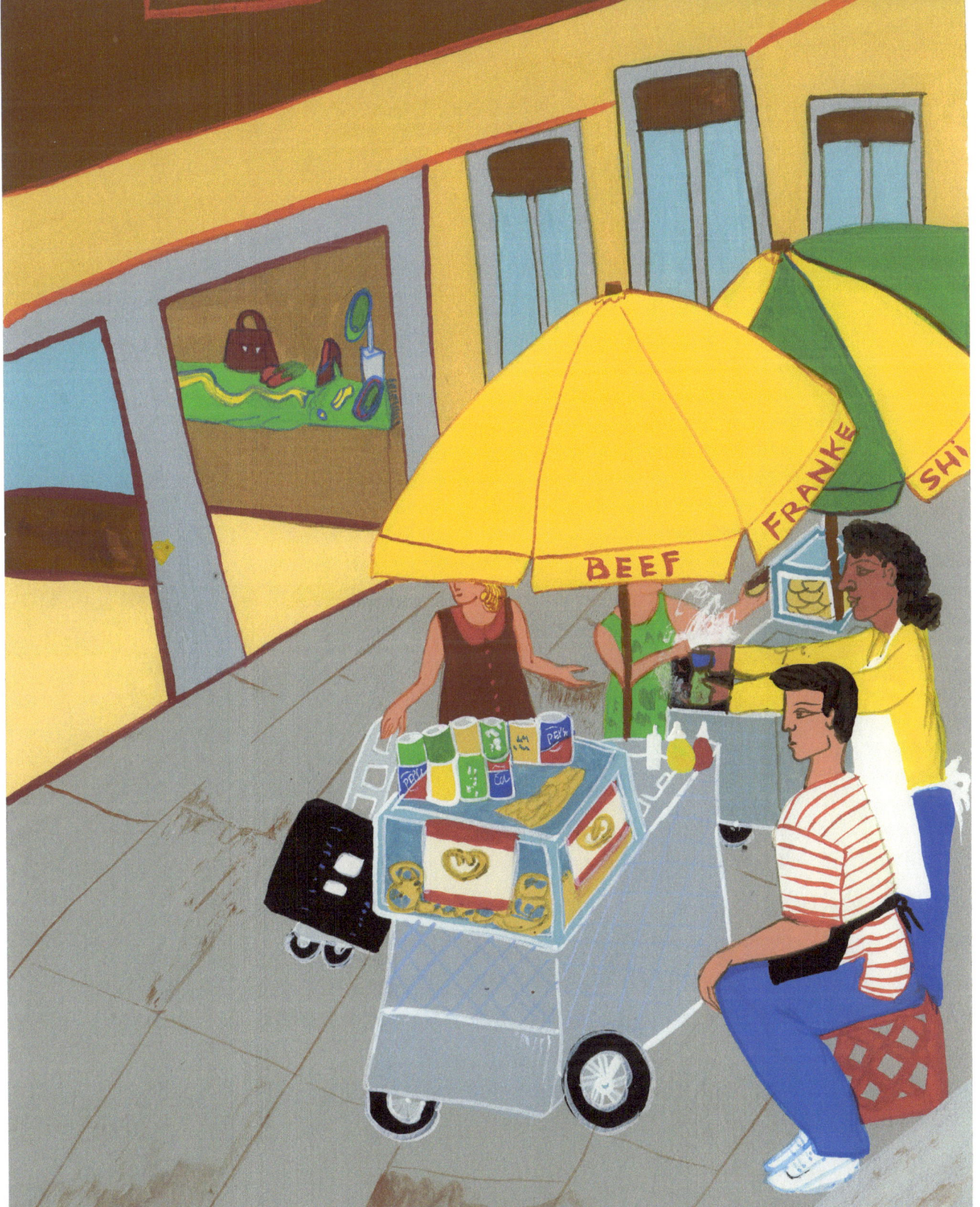

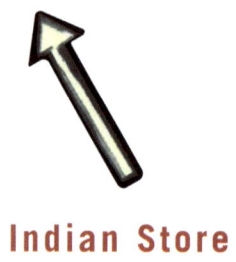

**Indian Store**

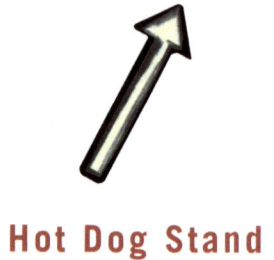

**Hot Dog Stand**

**Big Apple Circus**

8

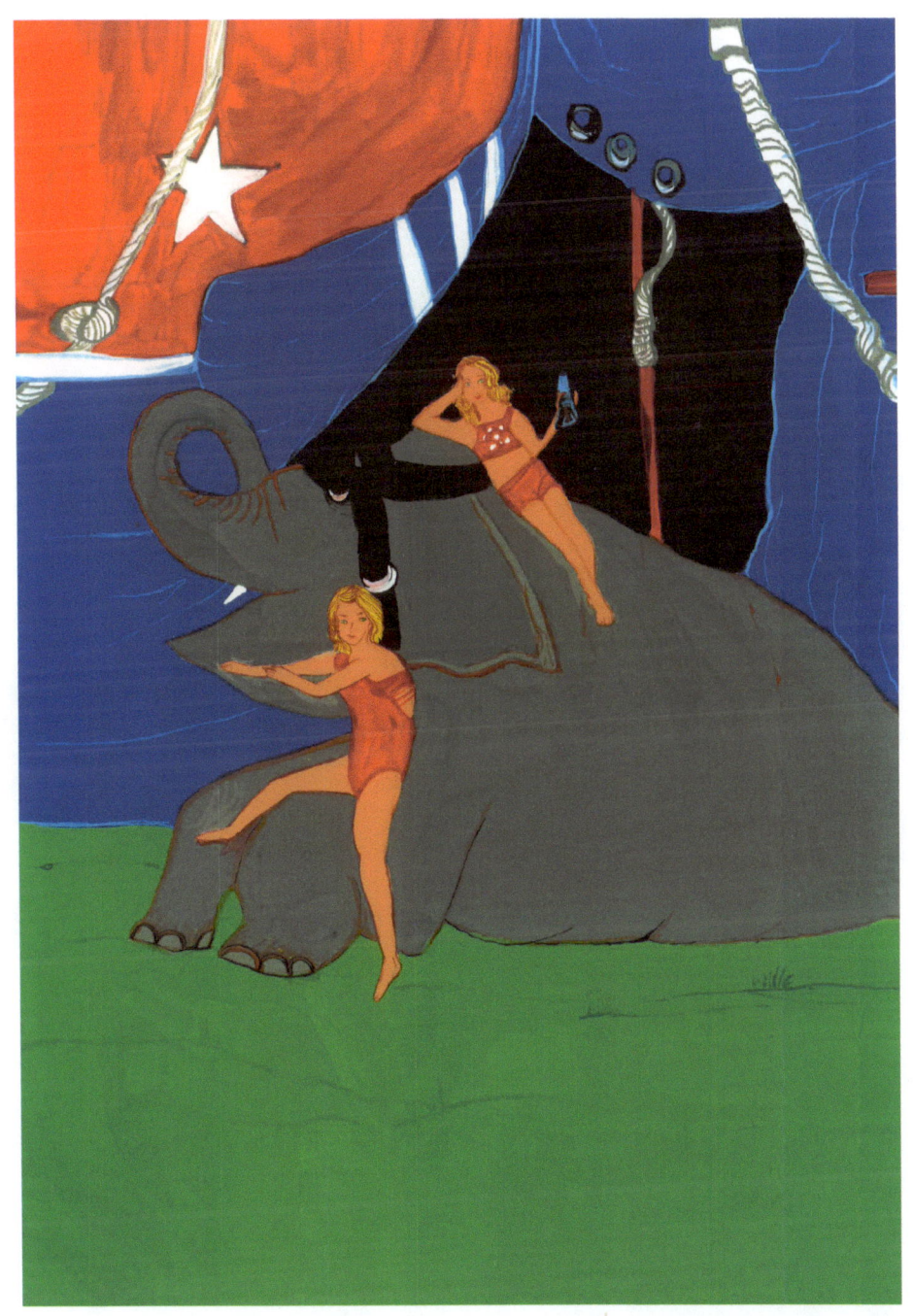

Gandhi, Union Square

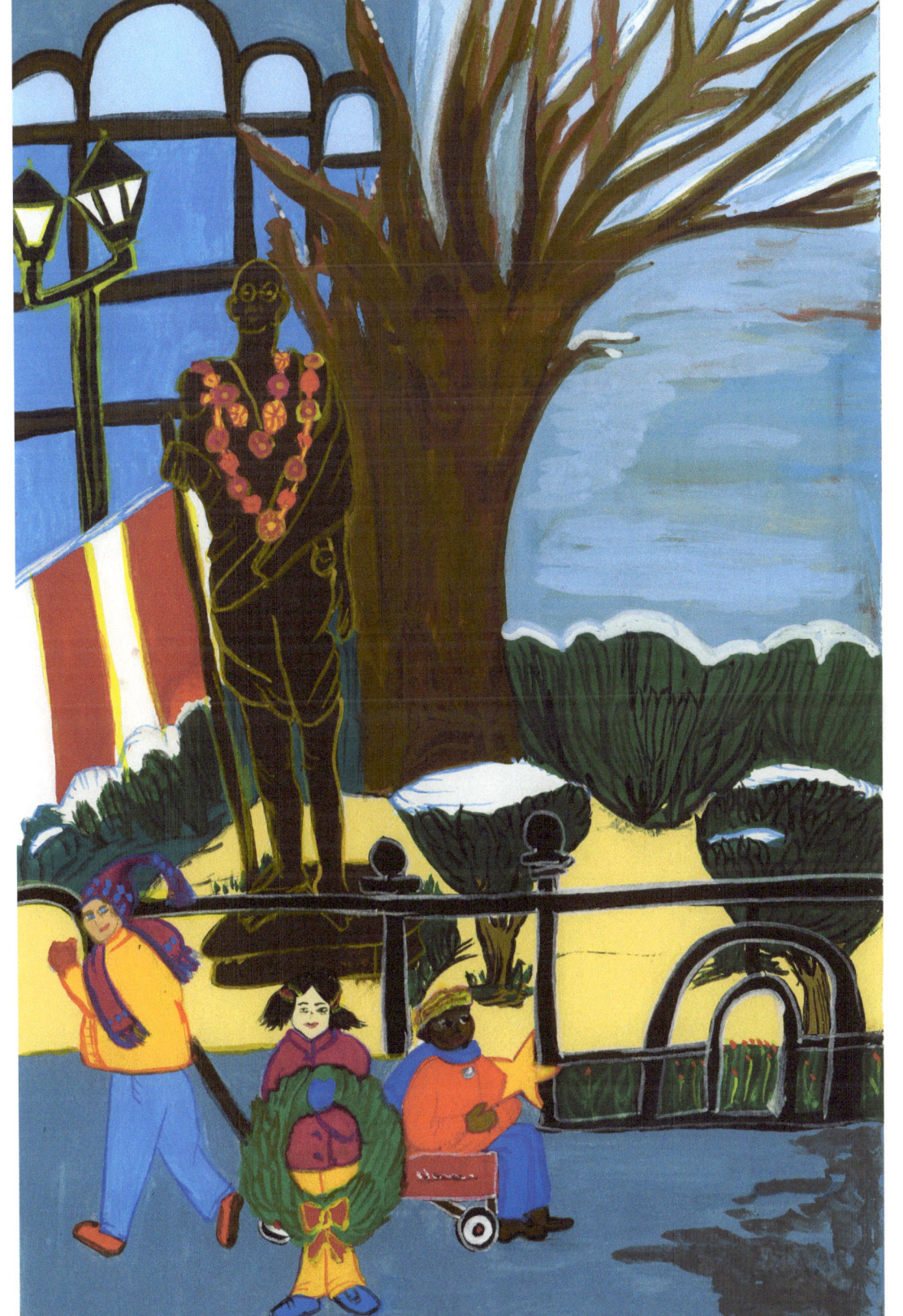

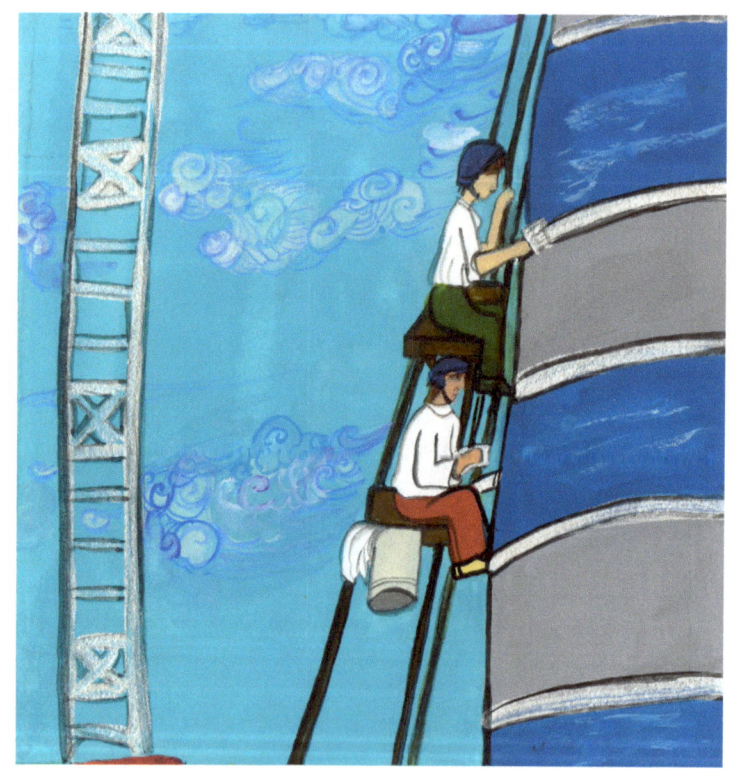

**Window Washers**

**Construction**

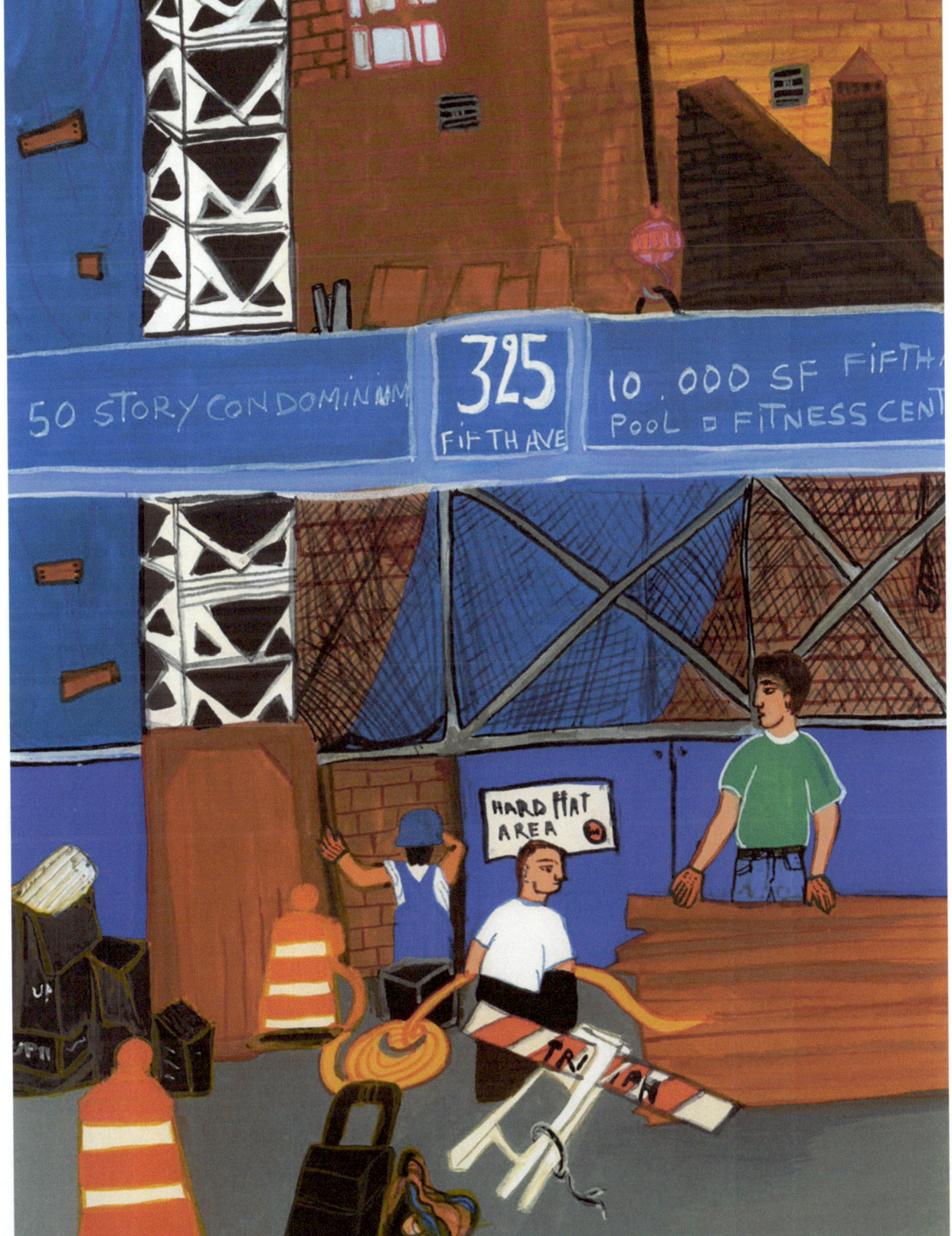

13

Y.M.C.A.

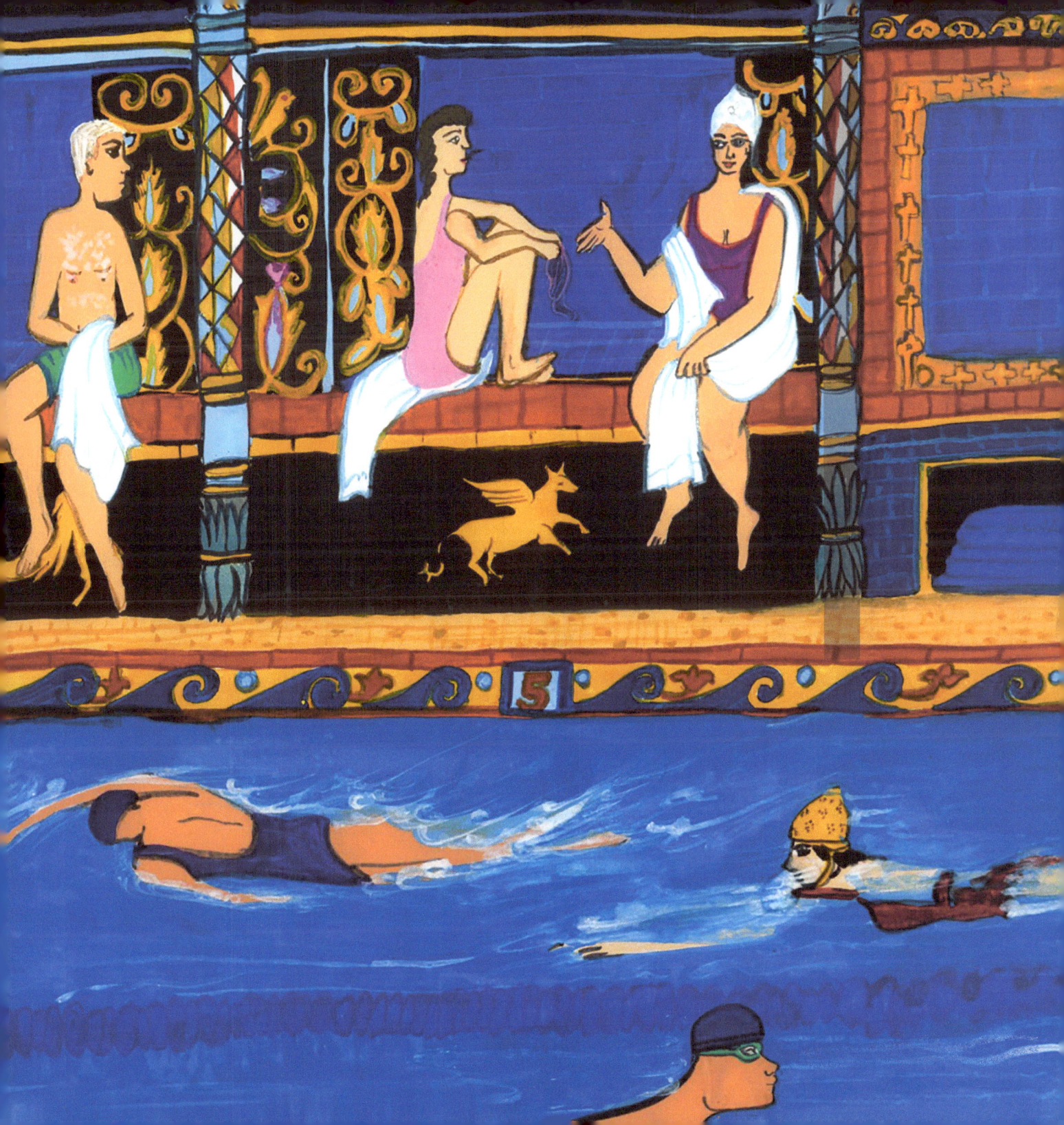

# Kundalini Yoga

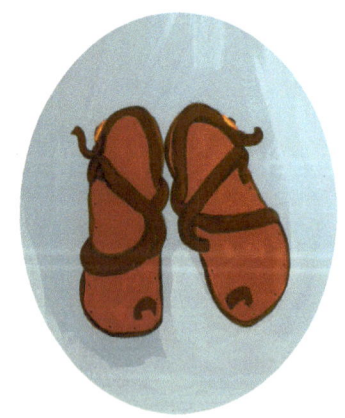

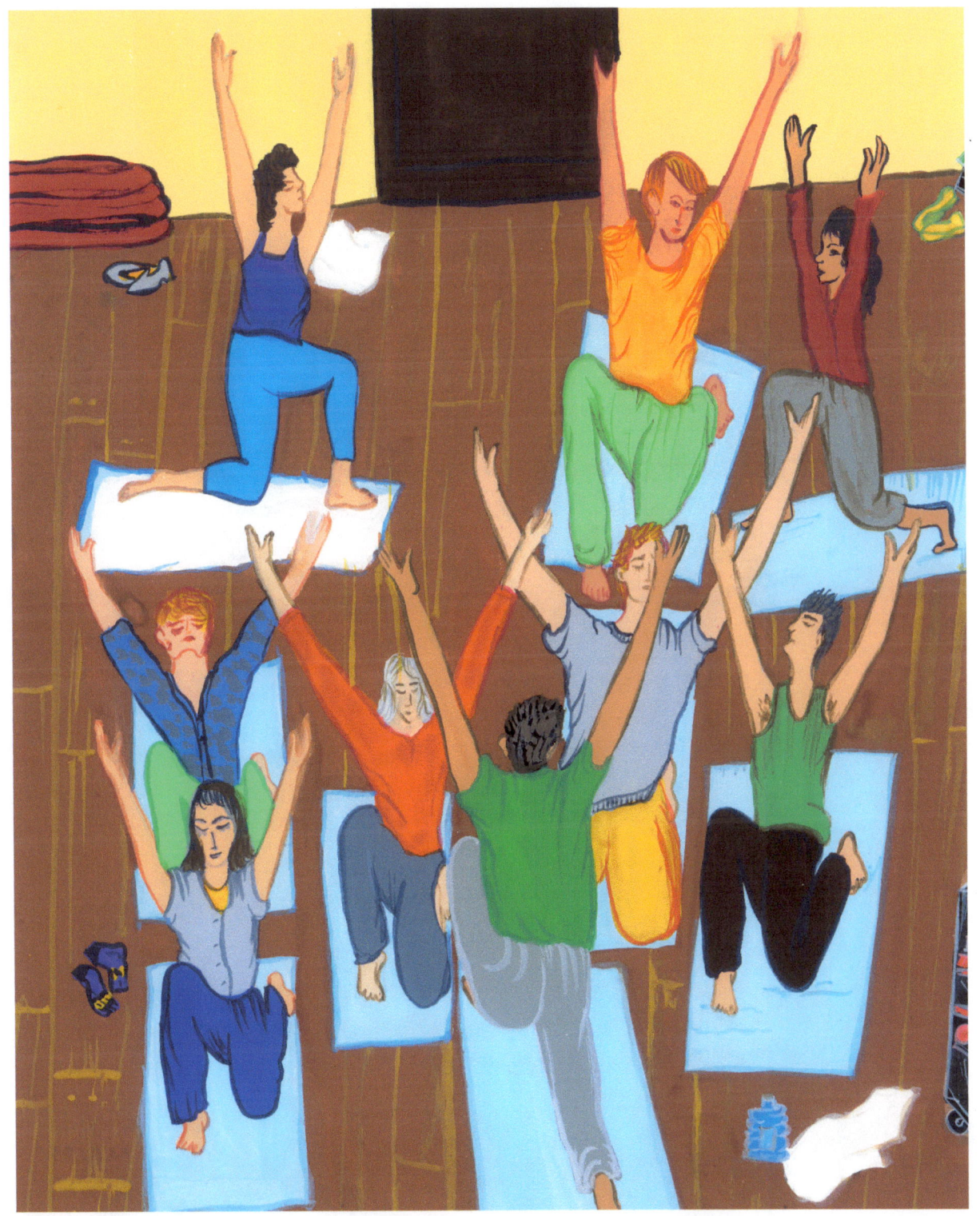

17

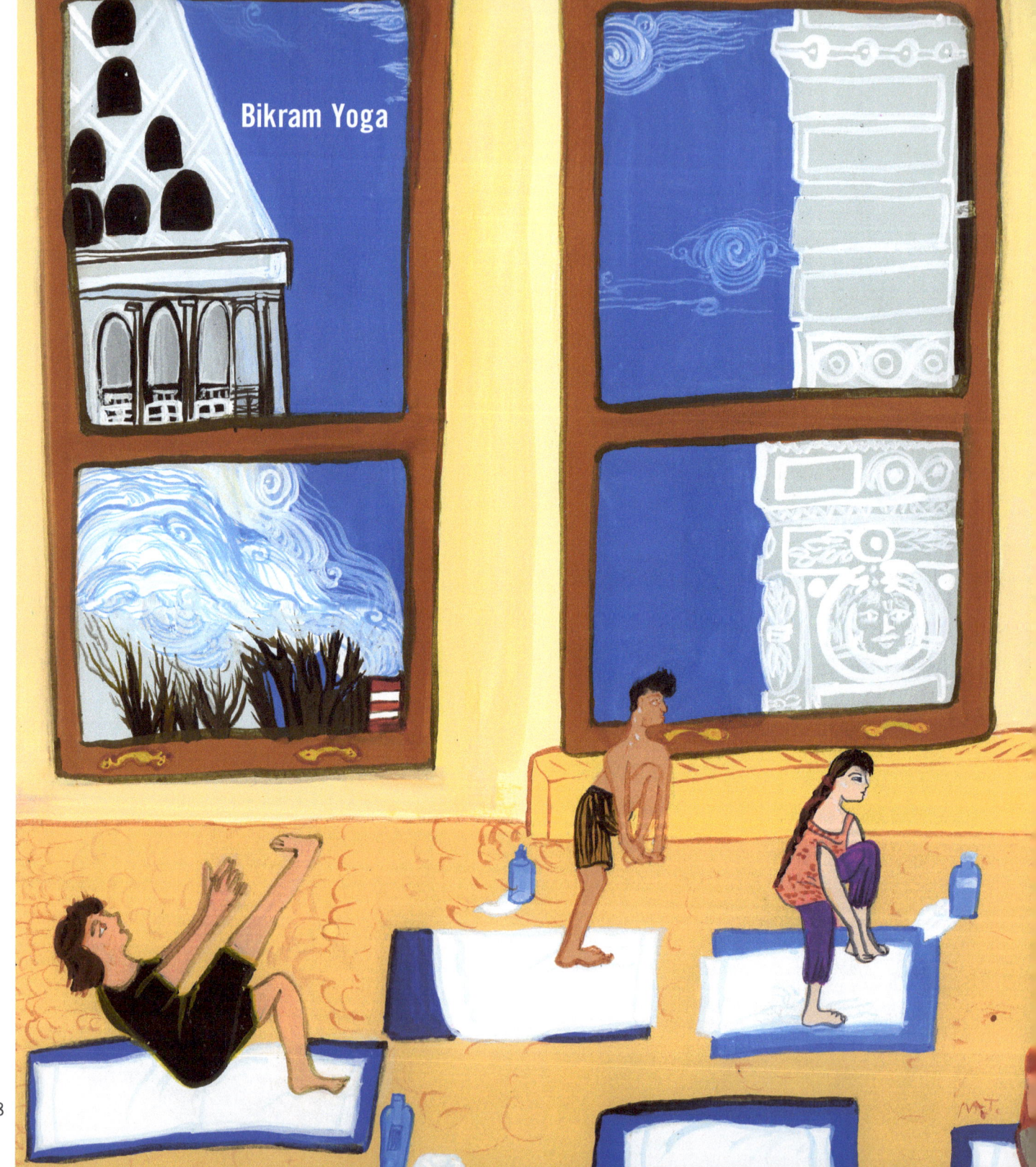

Bikram Yoga

18

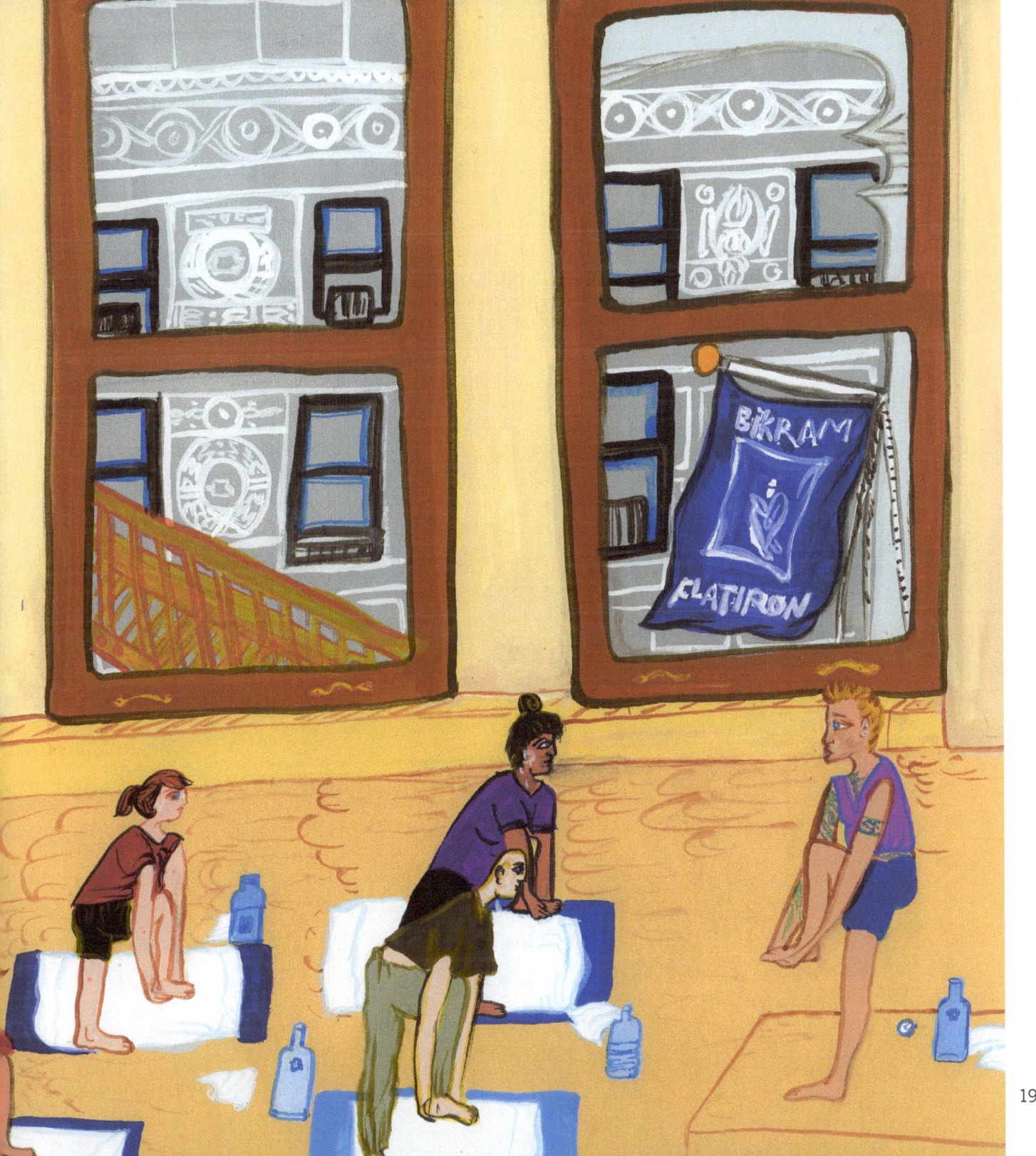

BIG CUP CAFÉ

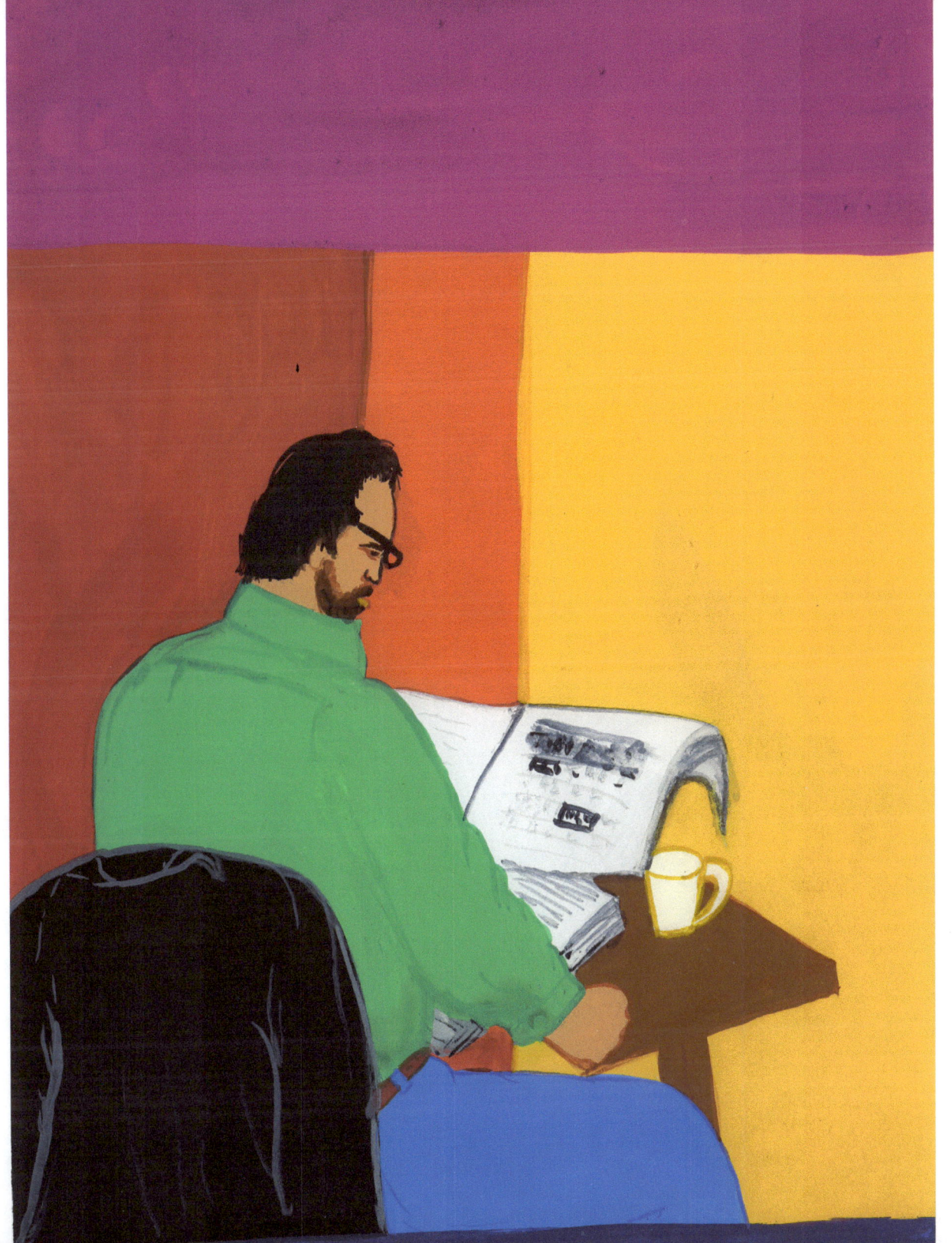

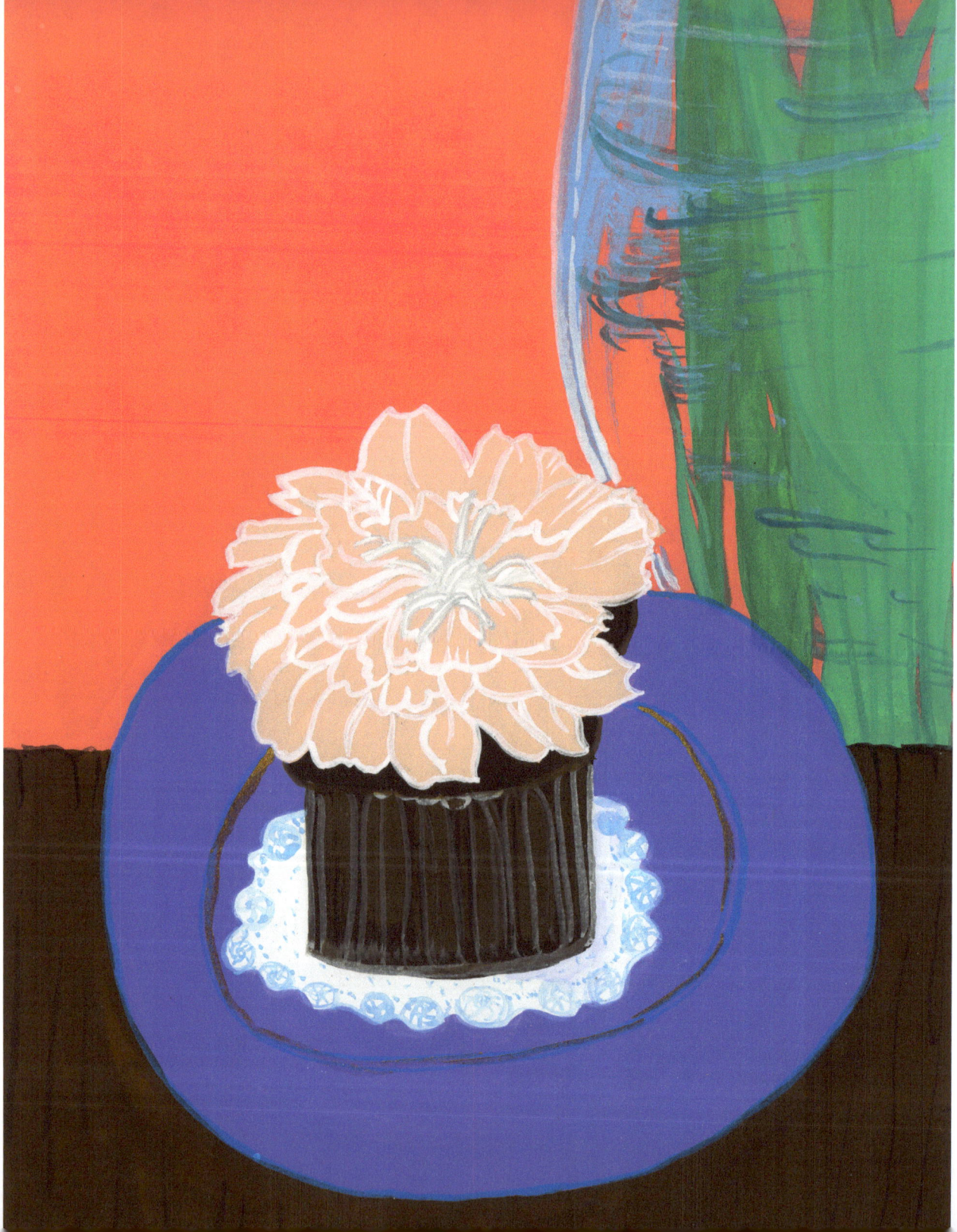

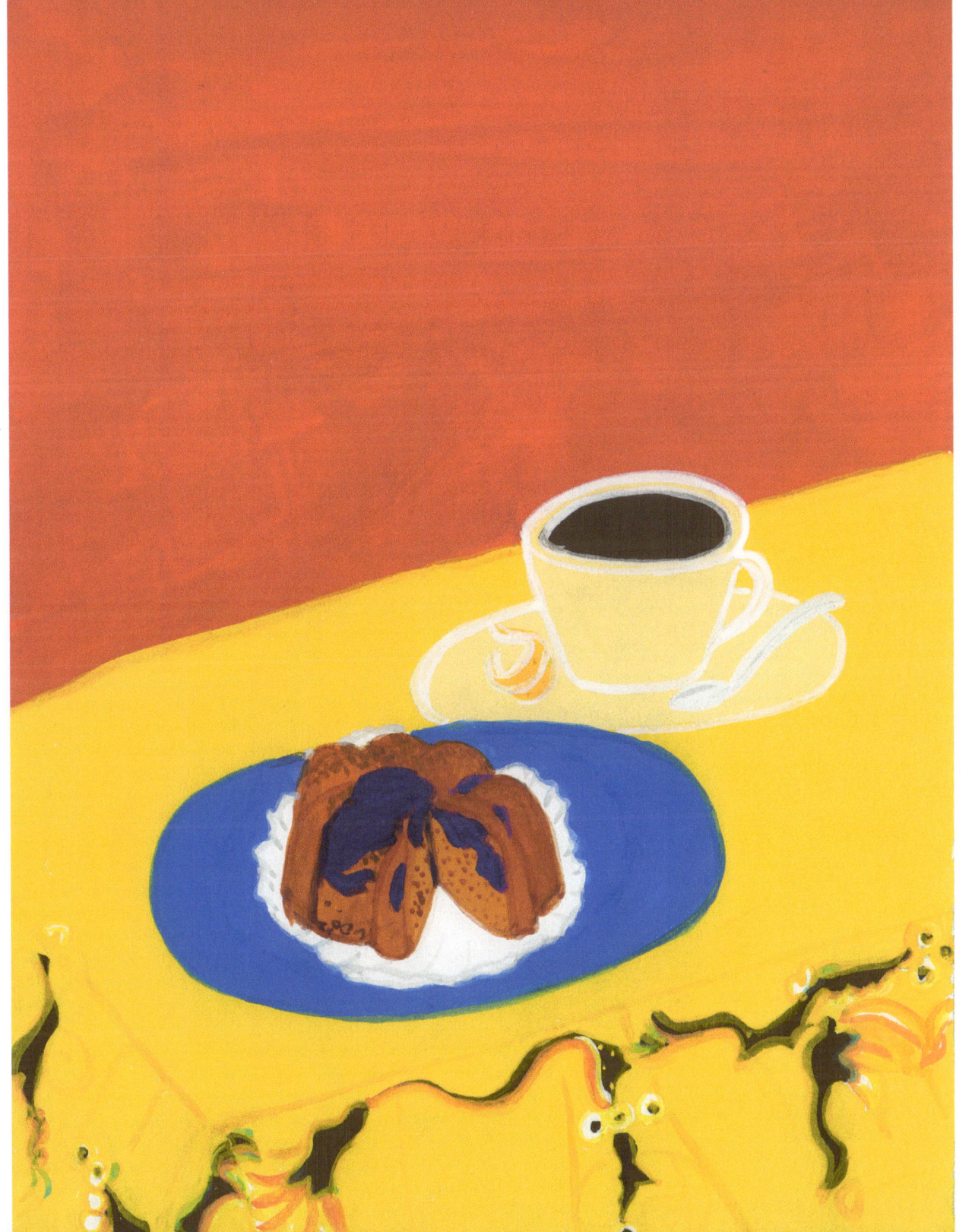

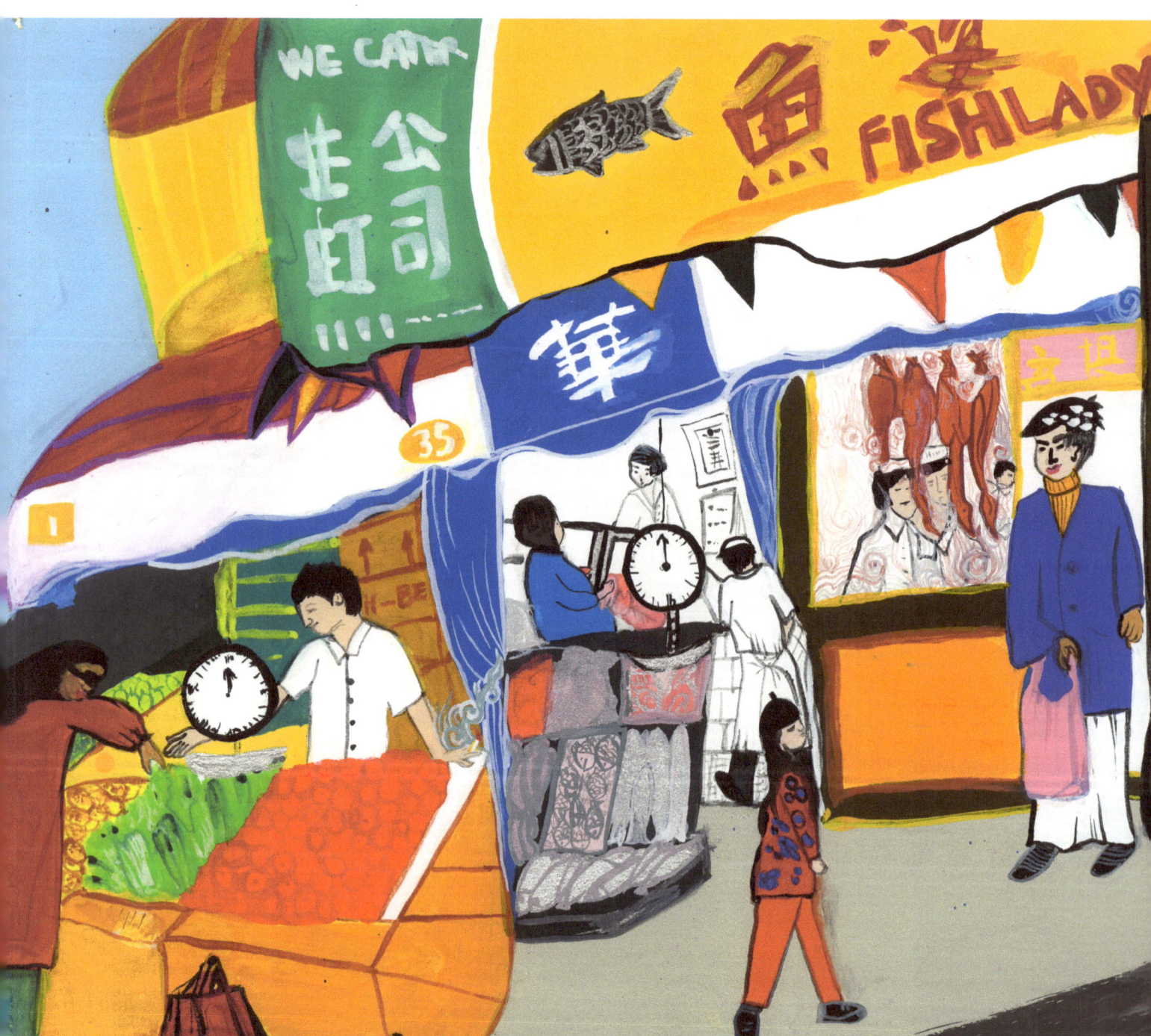

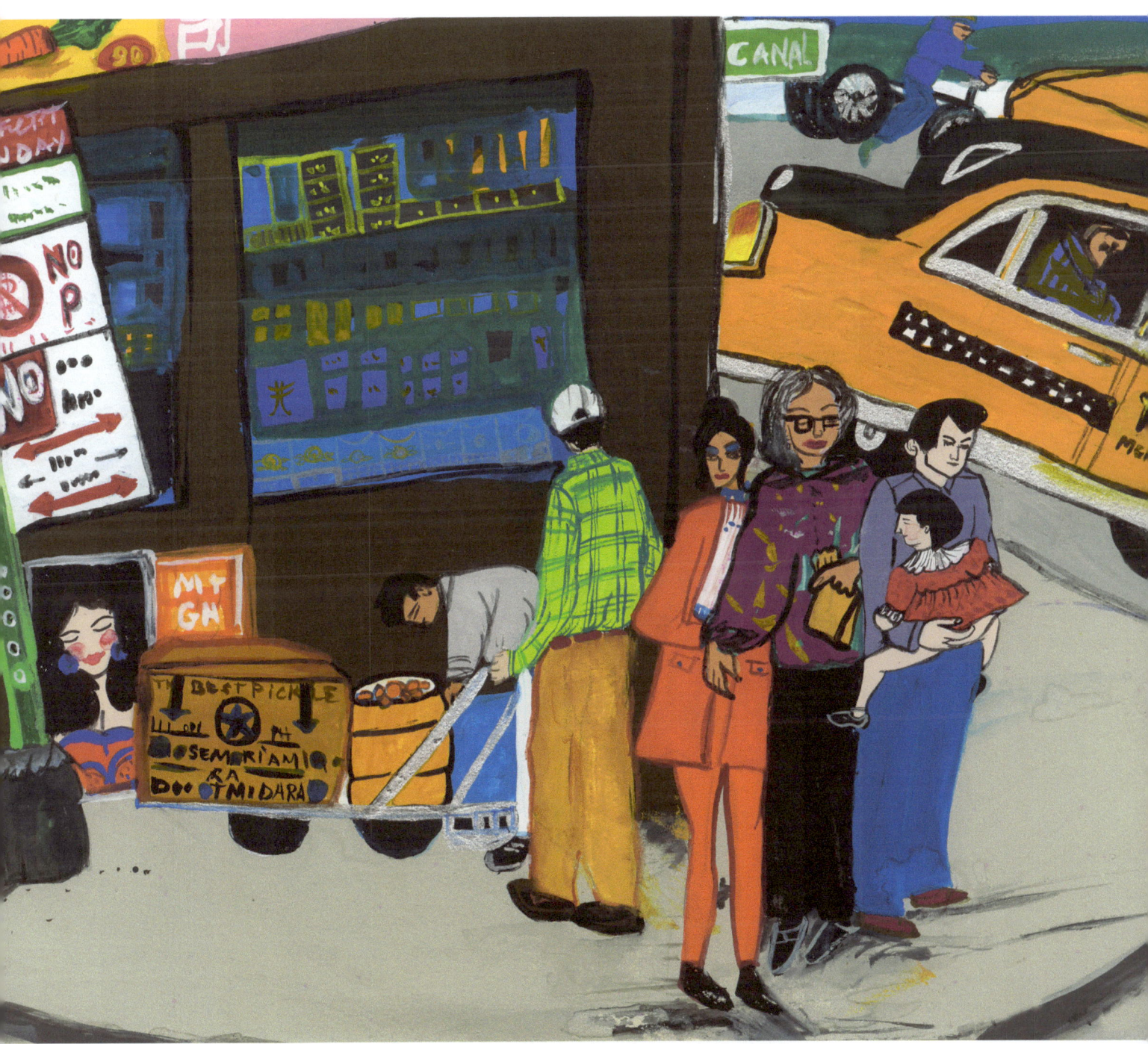

Chinatown

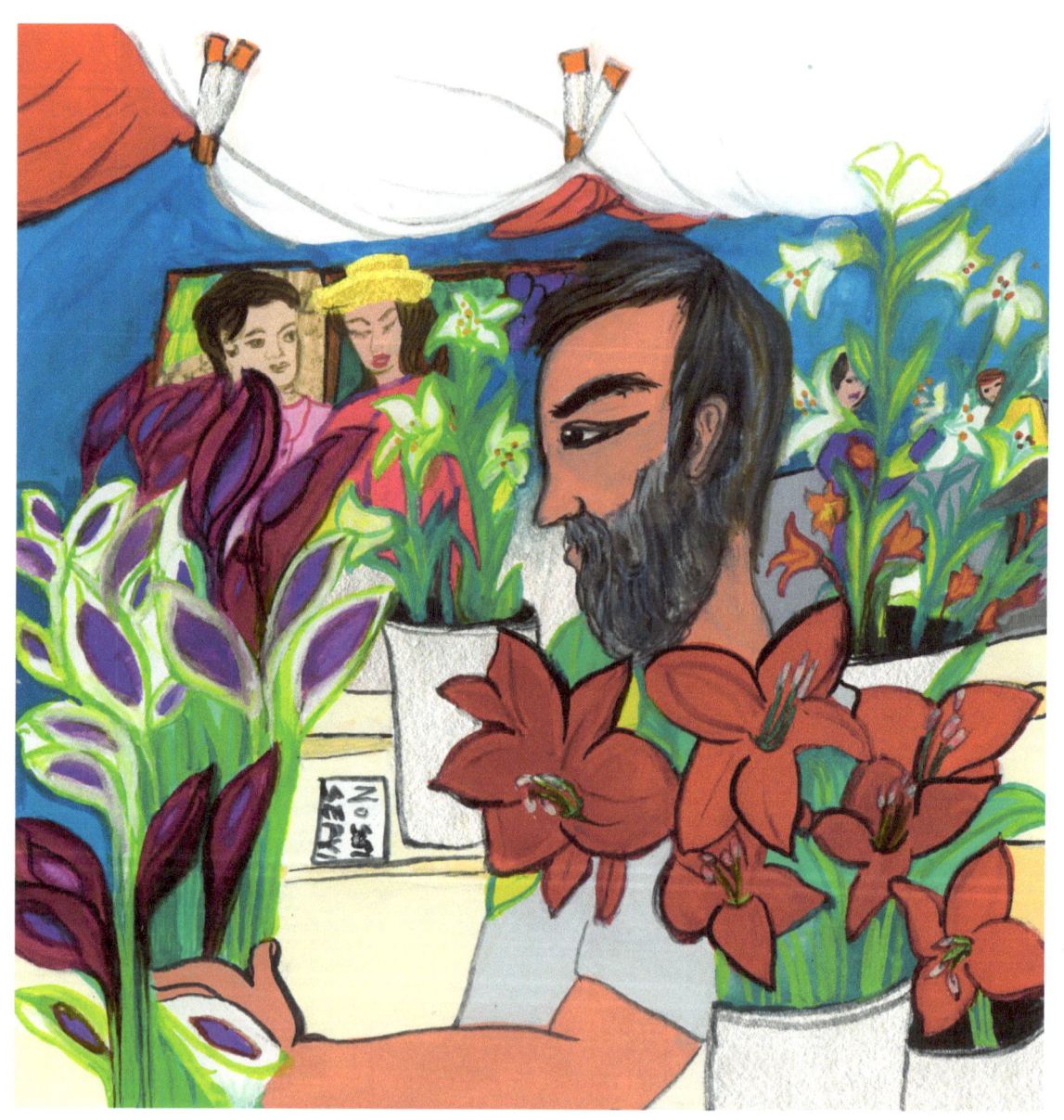

**Farmer's Market, Union Square**

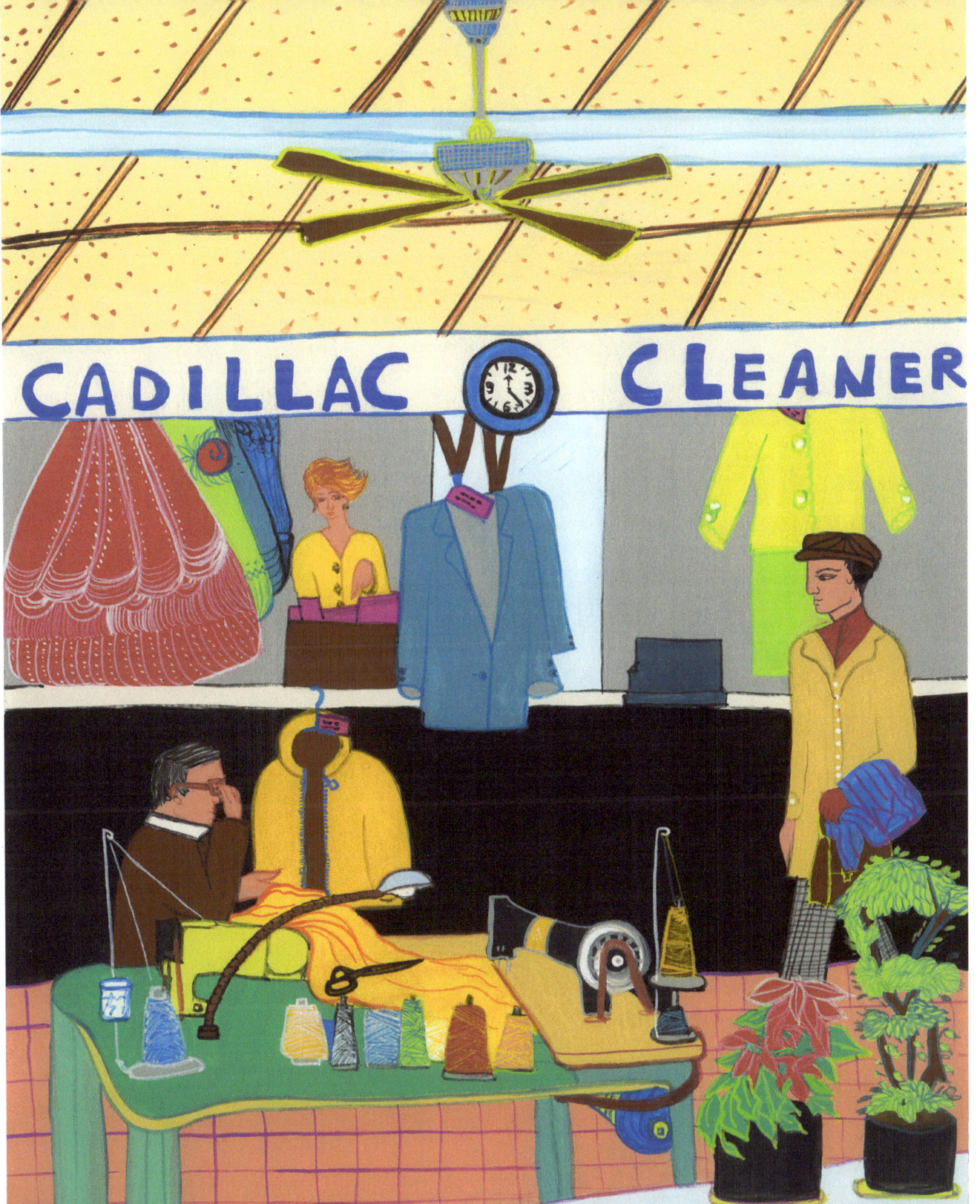

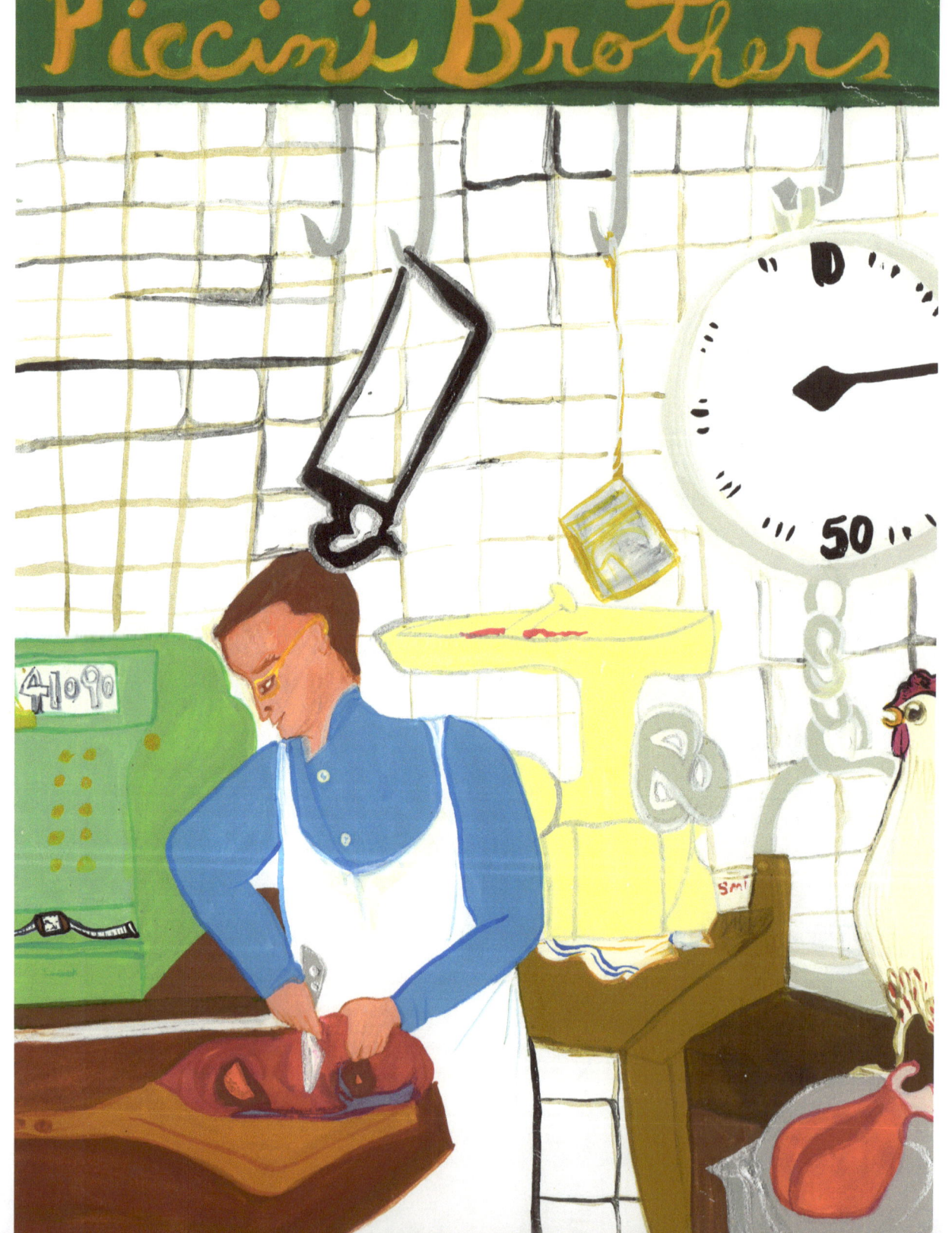

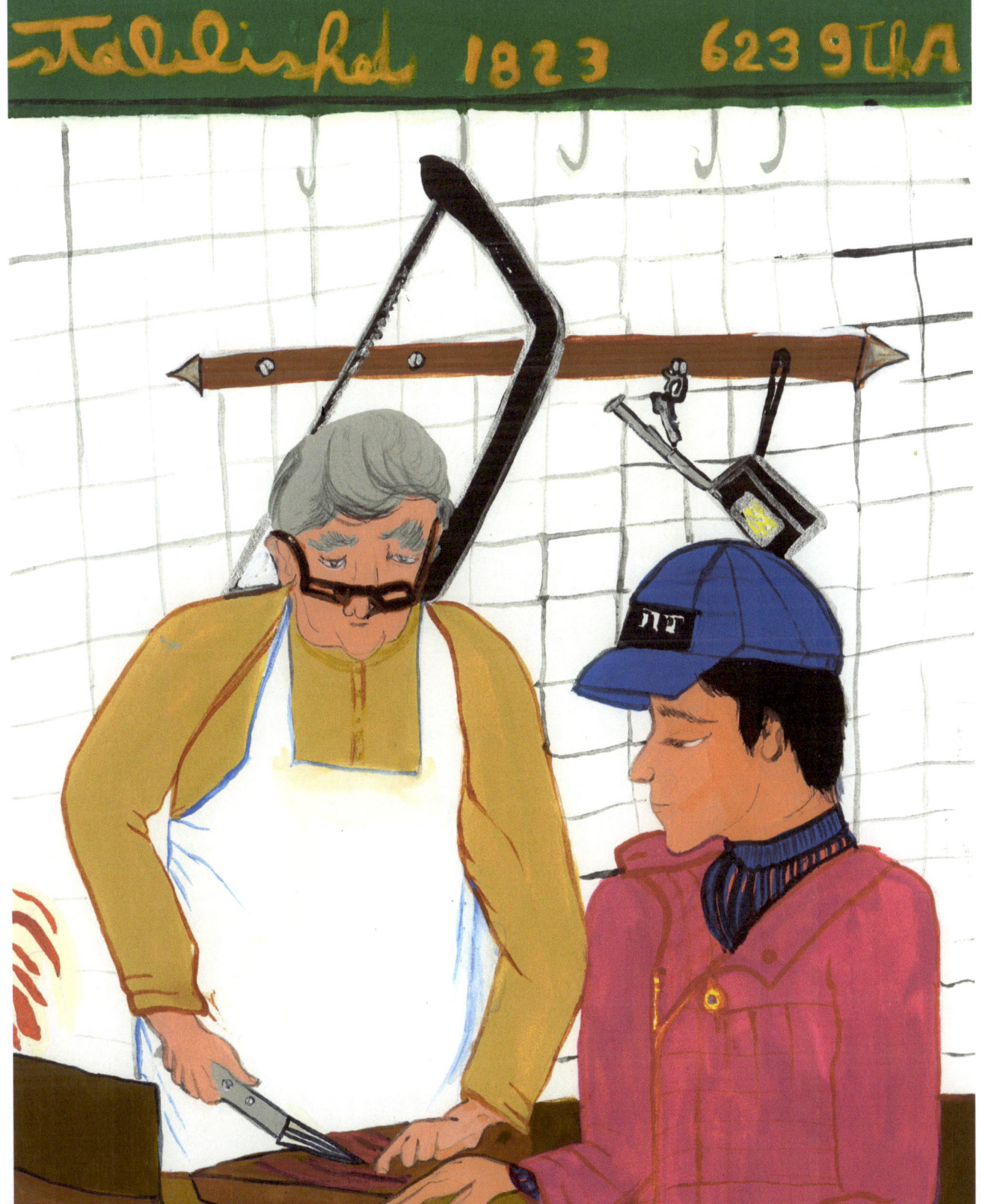

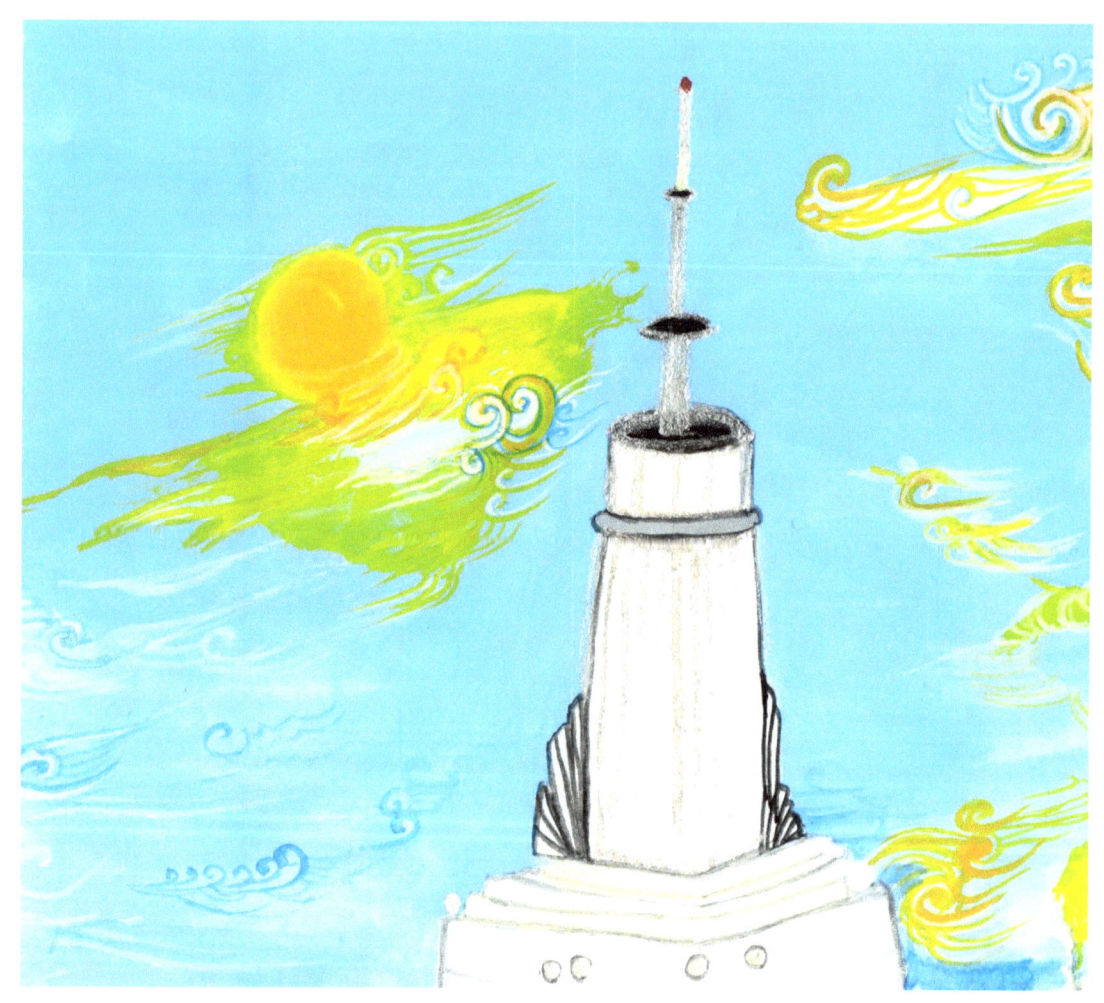

**Empire State Building Day and Night**

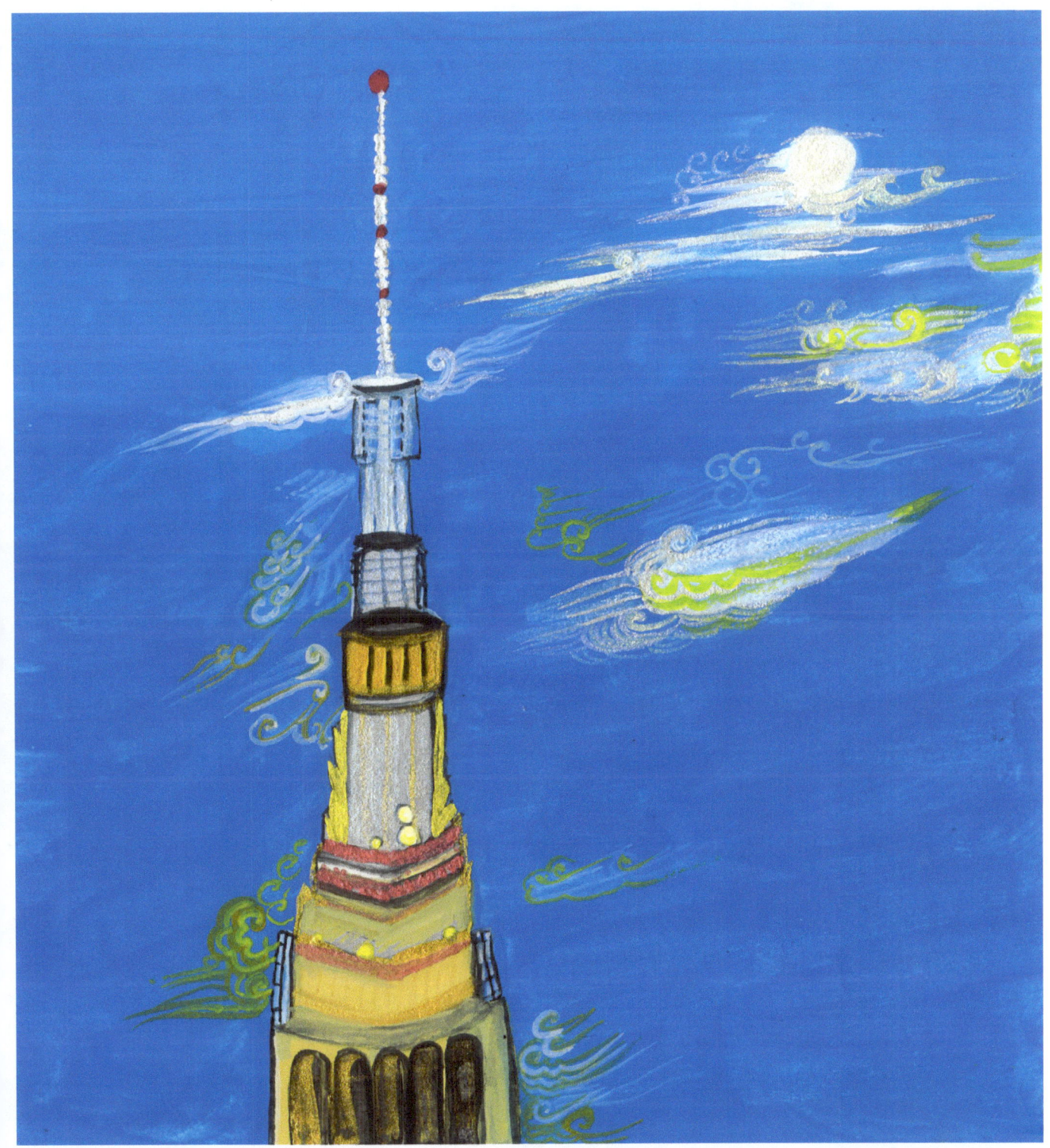

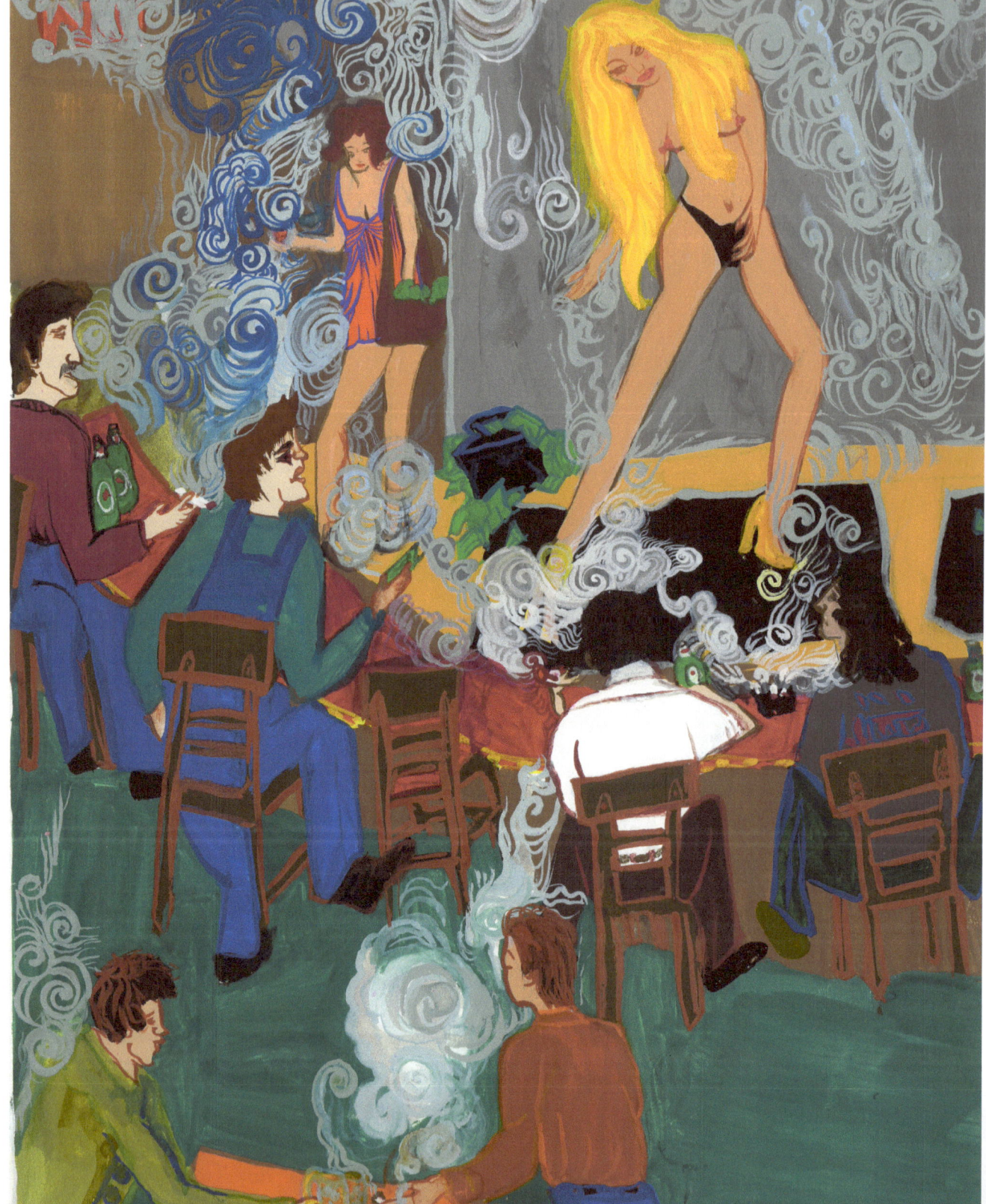

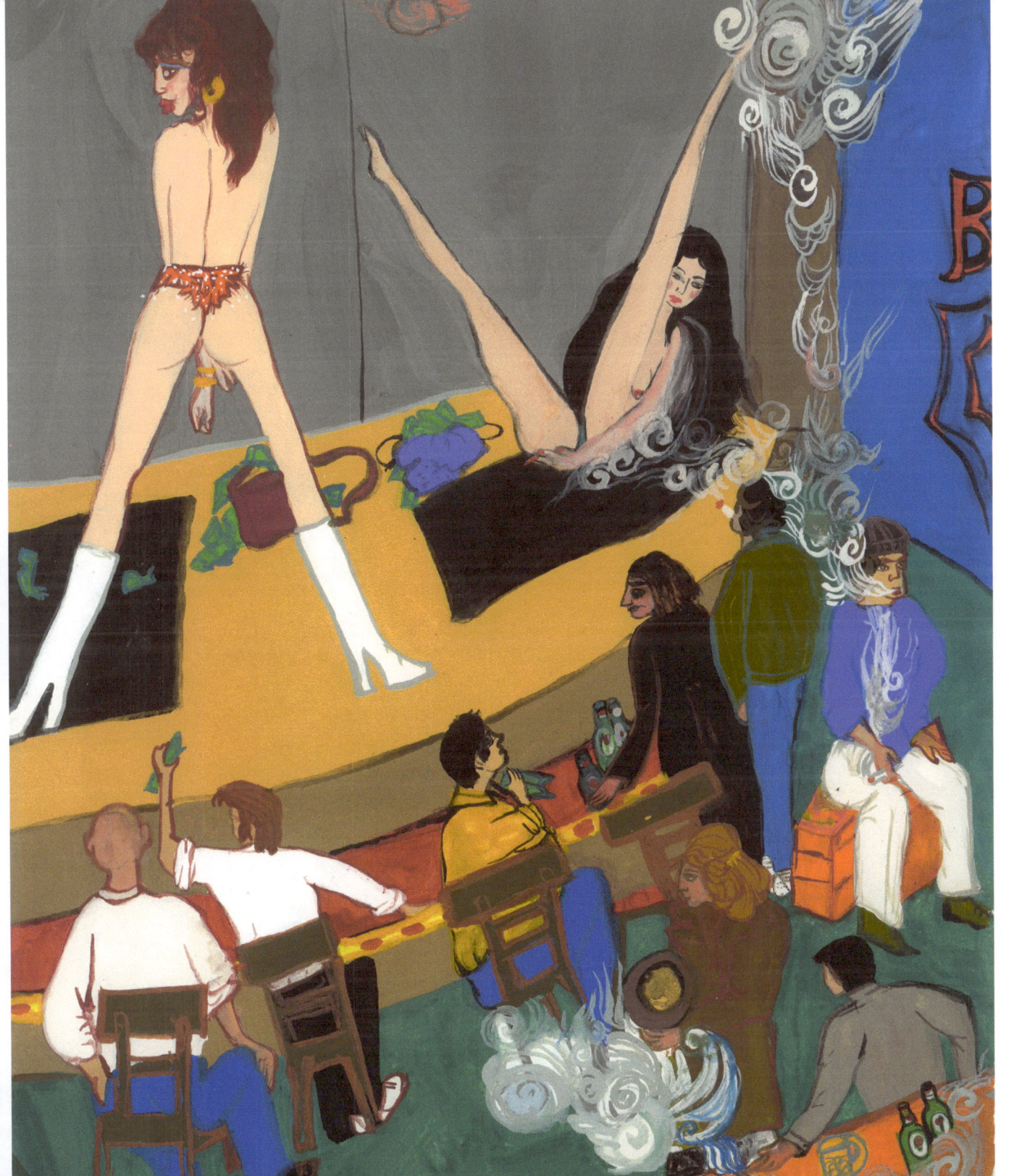

33

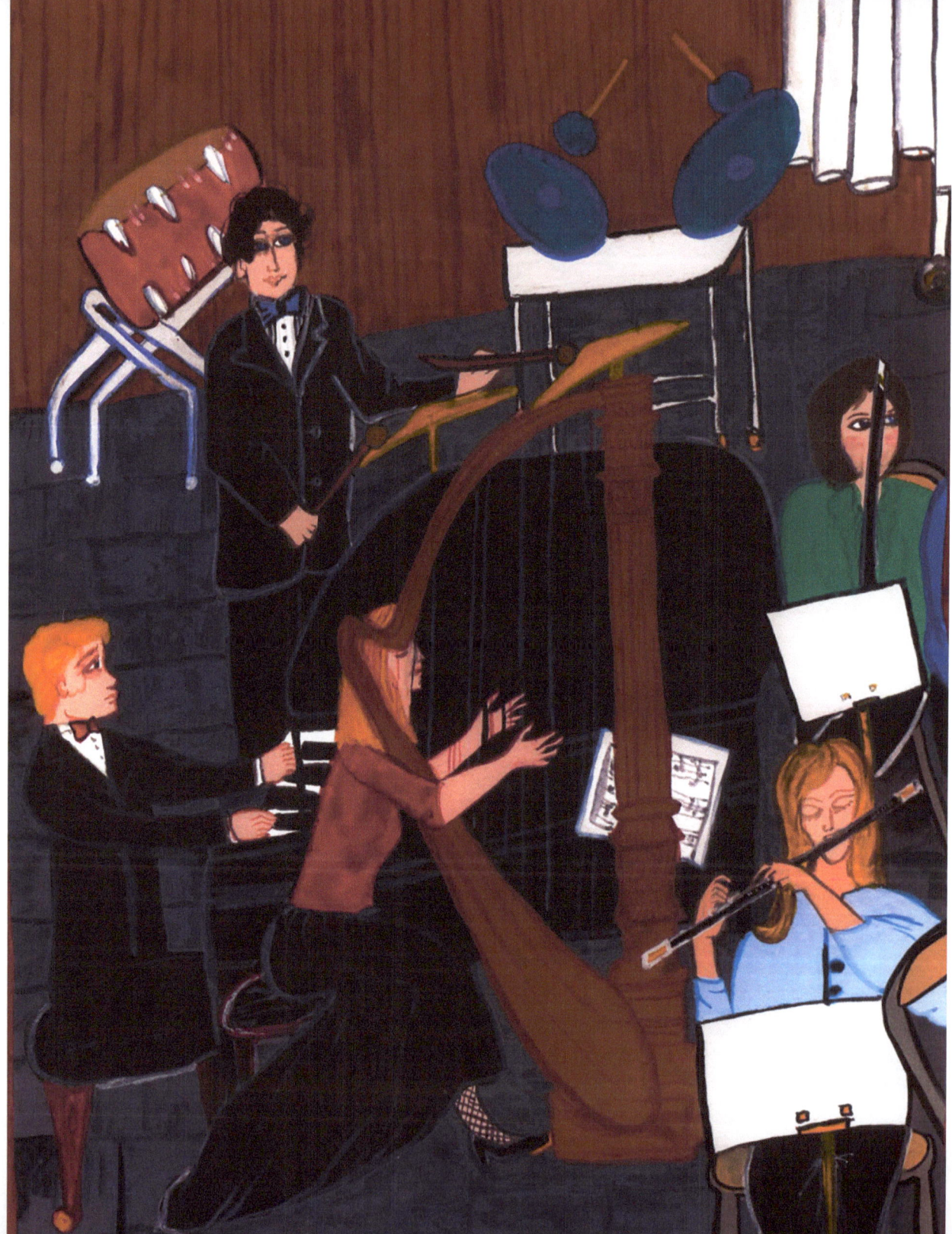

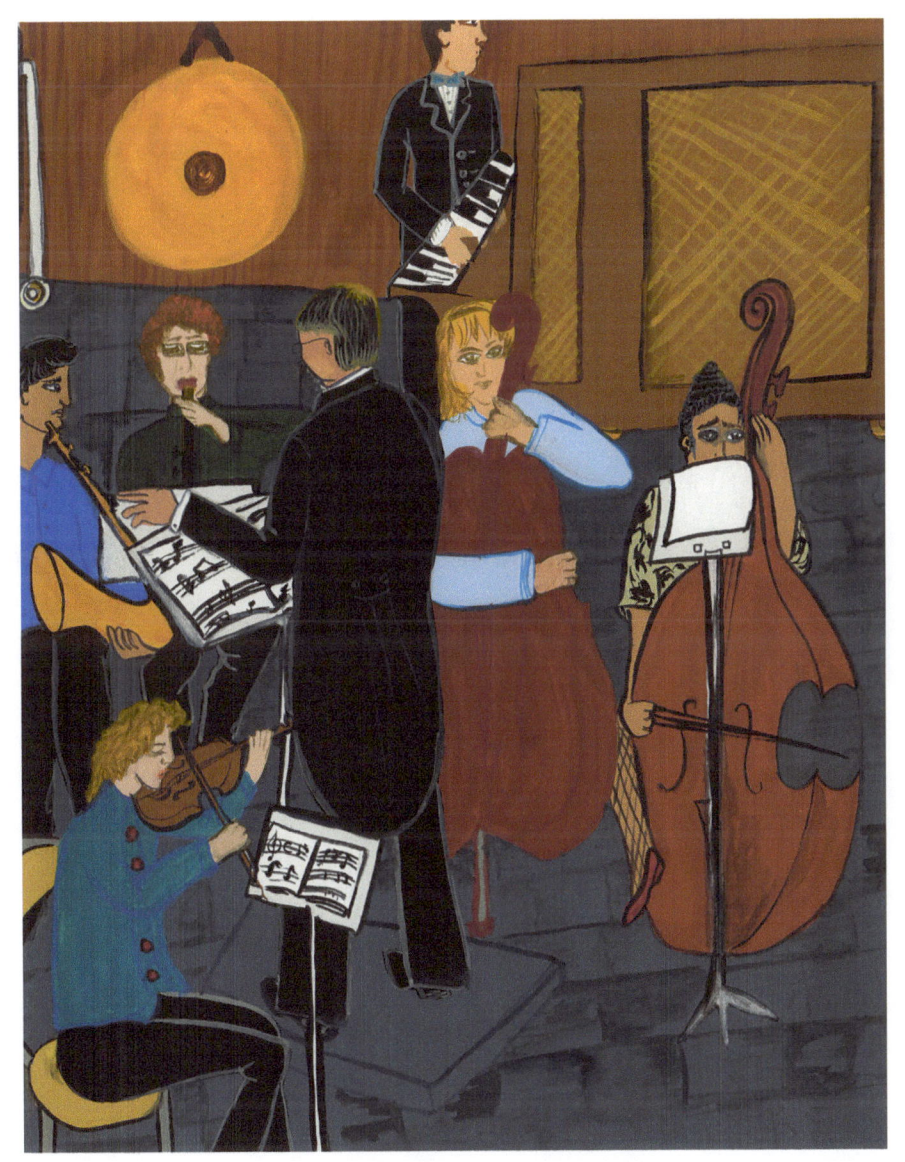

**Julliard Students**

# Lunch Break, Bryant Park

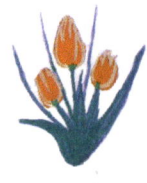

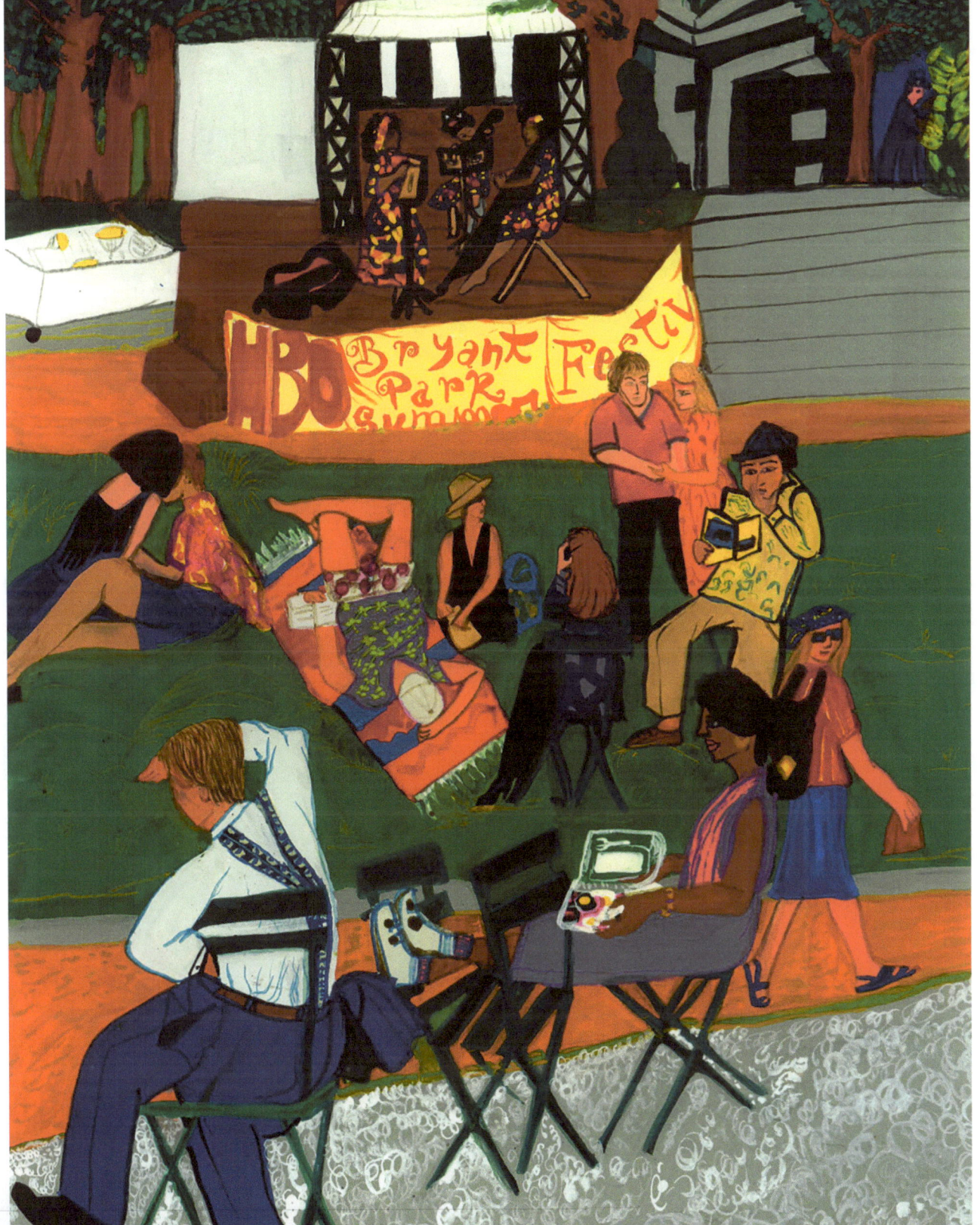

Empire Cinema

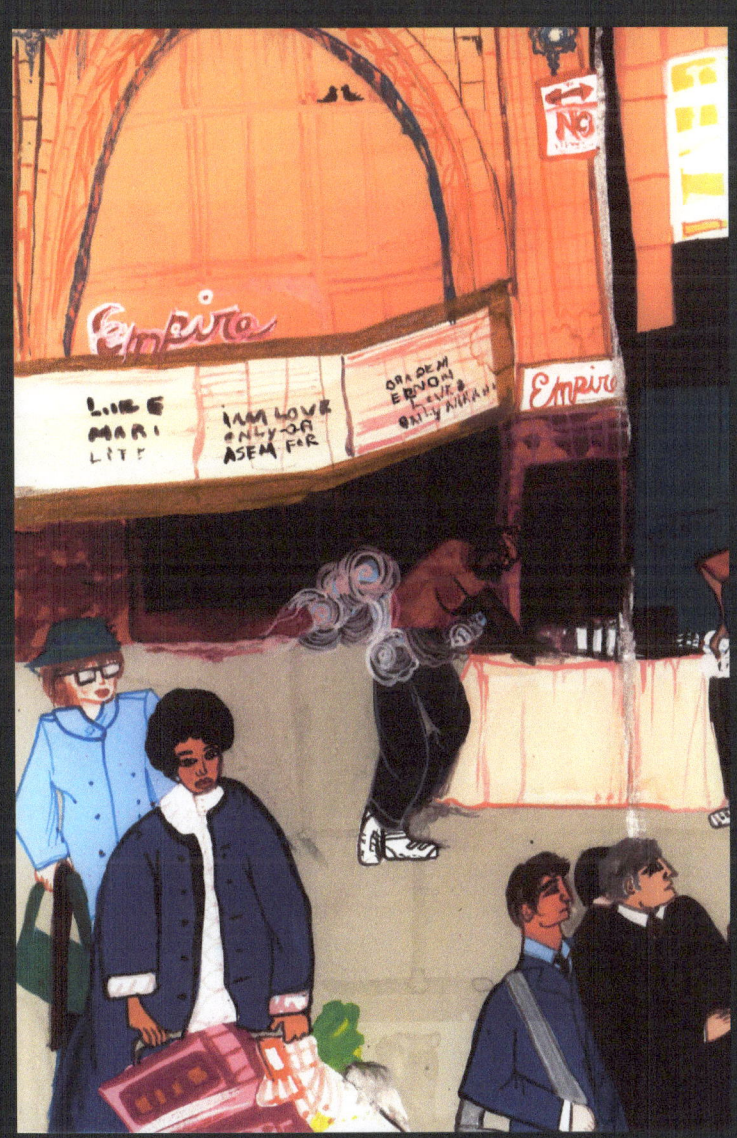

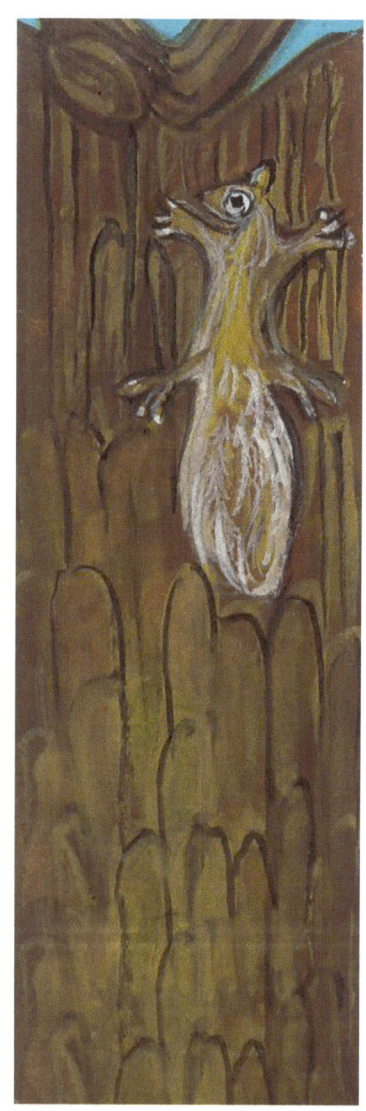

**Another City Pet**

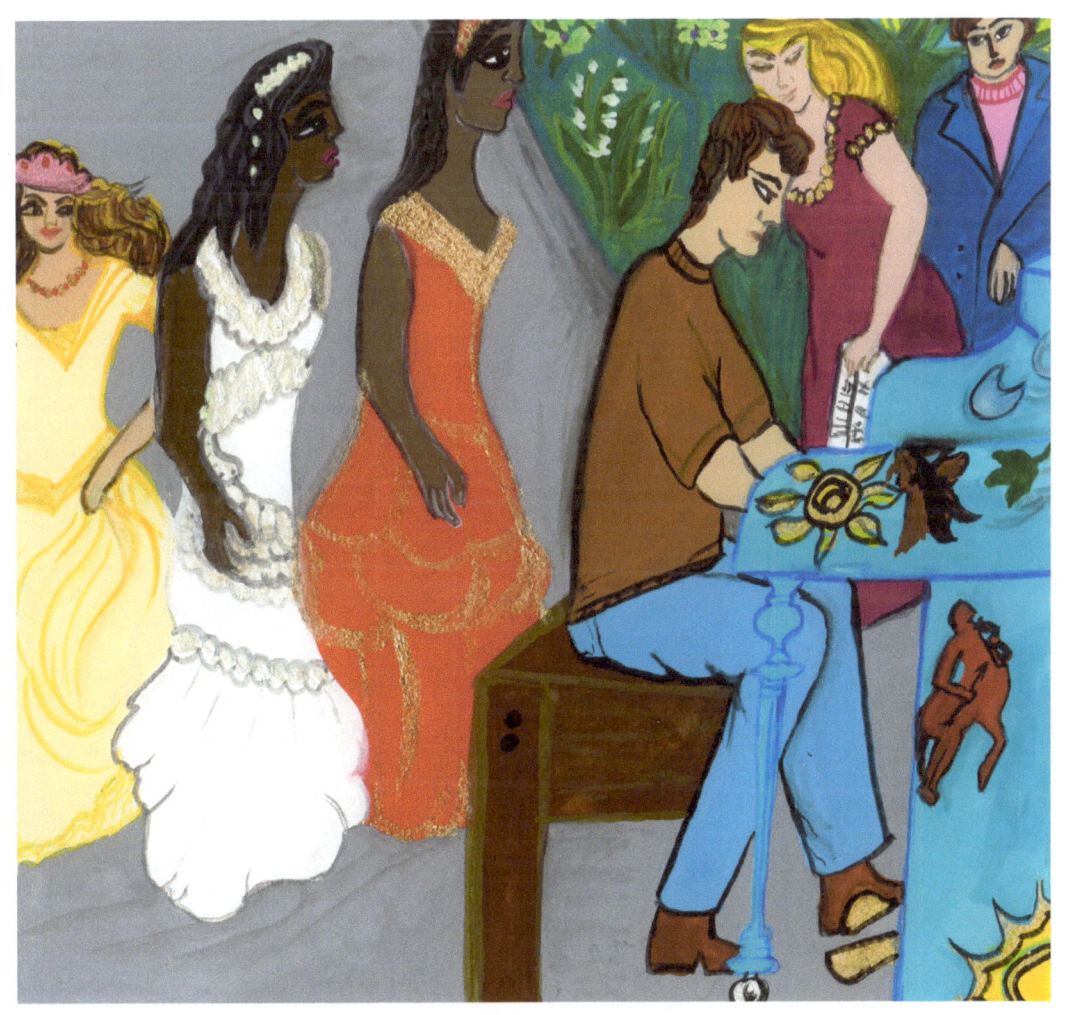

Opera, Madison Square Park

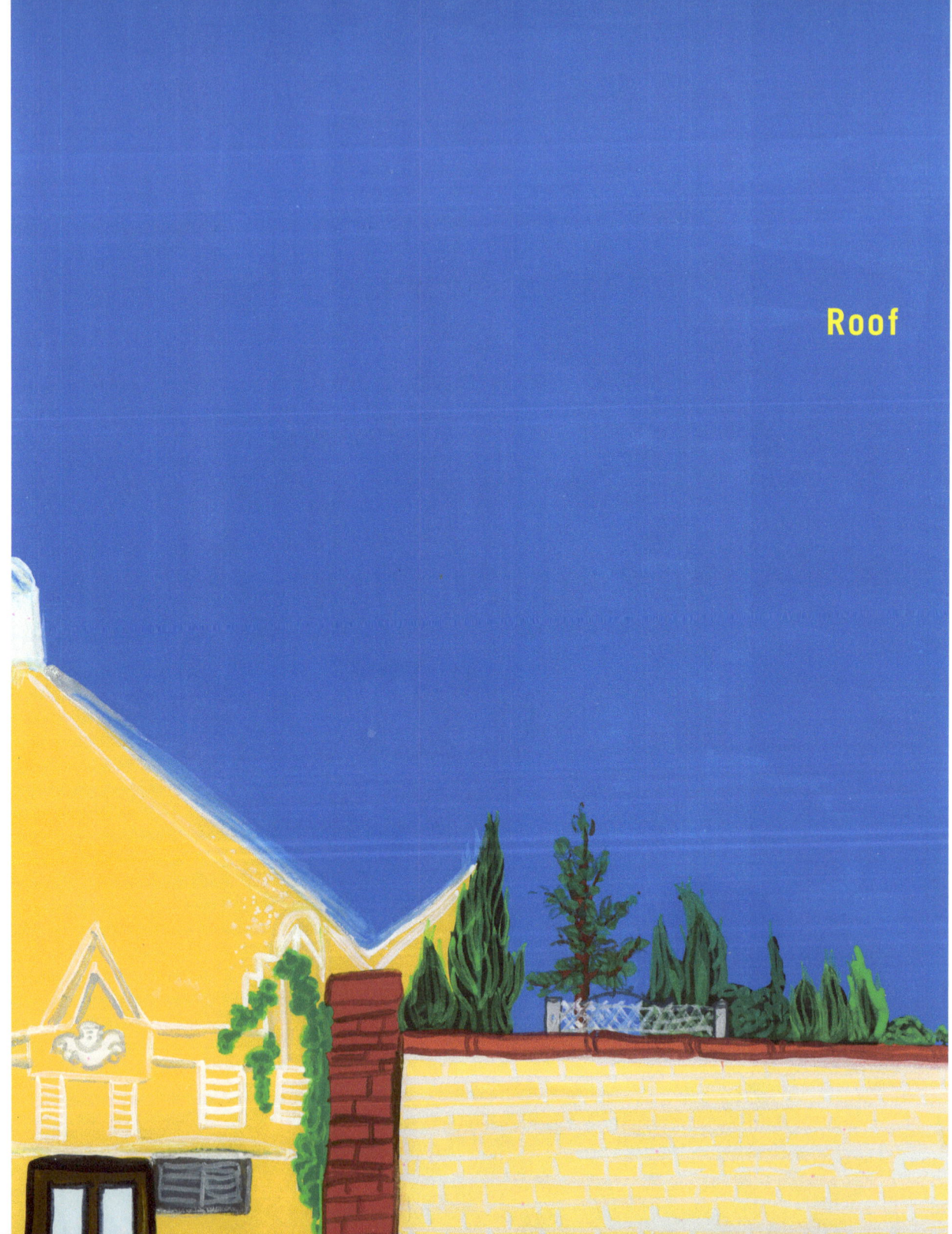

Roof

Gardens

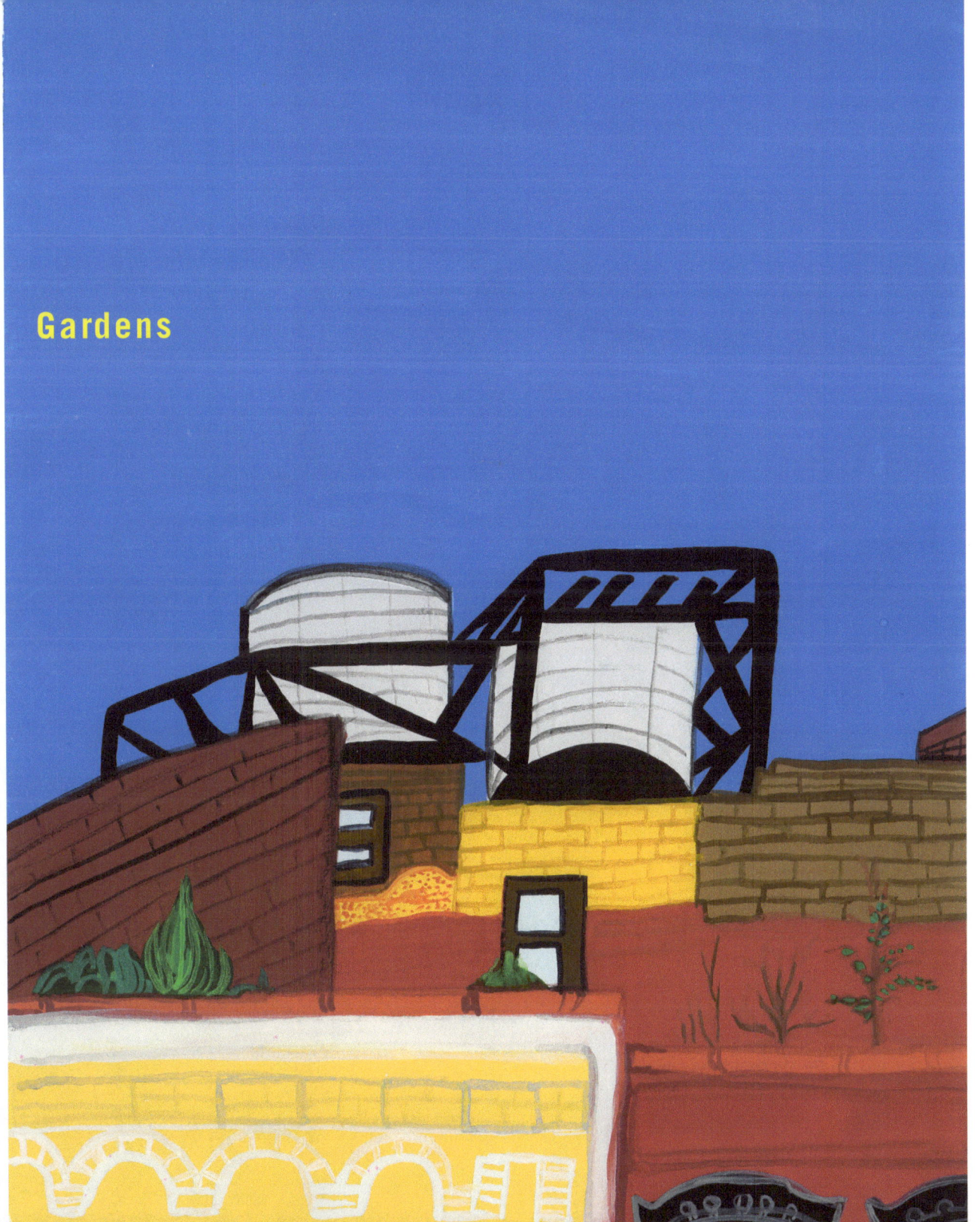

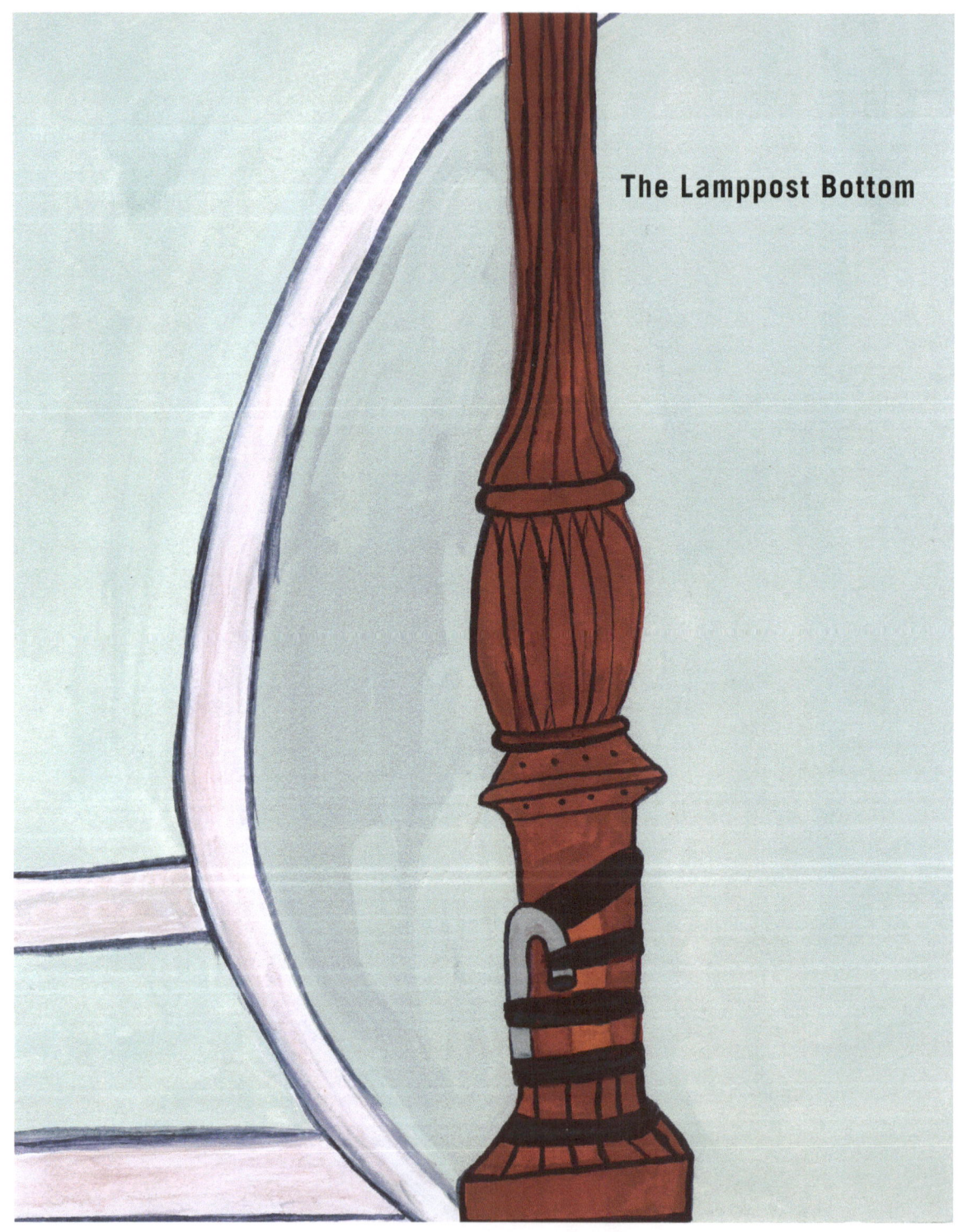

The Lamppost Bottom

Mariam Touzie was born in Tehran, Iran. She graduated from
Tehran University in Fine Arts. She then moved to New York City,
continuing her studies at the School of Visual Arts where she received
her masters degree and was awarded the Paula Rhodes prize
for exquisite artwork.

Her books include, narrative illustrated *Rostram the Warrior*
(available on blurb.com).
Series of narrative illustrated books
*"Chronicles of Seemorgh & The Three Warriors"*
consisting of three books —*"Birth", "Love" and "Baby"*
She also illustrated a digital book *"Florida on a Magic Carpet"*
(all available on Amazon.com)

To learn more of her art works visit:
mariamtouzie.com
mariamtouzie.blogspot.com

www.ingramcontent.com/pod-product-compliance
Lightning Source LLC
Chambersburg PA
CBHW050900180526

45159CB00007B/2744